KT-226-265

WILL HUTTON

SAVING BRITAIN

ANDREW ADONIS

ABACUS

First published in Great Britain in 2018 by Abacus

1 3 5 7 9 10 8 6 4 2

Copyright © Will Hutton & Andrew Adonis 2018

The moral right of the authors has been asserted.

All rights reserved.
No part of this publication may be reproduced, stored in a
retrieval system, or transmitted, in any form or by any means, without
the prior permission in writing of the publisher, nor be otherwise circulated
in any form of binding or cover other than that in which it is published
and without a similar condition including this condition being
imposed on the subsequent purchaser.

A CIP catalogue record for this book
is available from the British Library.

ISBN 978-1-4087-1122-4

Typeset in Caslon by M Rules
Printed and bound in Great Britain by
Clays Ltd, Elcograf S.p.A

Papers used by Abacus are from well-managed forests
and other responsible sources.

Abacus
An imprint of
Little, Brown Book Group
Carmelite House
50 Victoria Embankment
London EC4Y 0DZ

An Hachette UK Company
www.hachette.co.uk

www.littlebrown.co.uk

Will Hutton is principal of Hertford College, Oxford, co-founder of Big Innovation Centre and columnist for the *Observer*, where he was editor, then editor-in-chief for four years. His career in journalism included being economics editor for BBC 2's *Newsnight* and then the *Guardian*.

Andrew Adonis is a Labour member of the House of Lords and visiting professor at King's College London. As Transport Secretary he pioneered HS2 and Crossrail; as Minister for Schools he forged Teach First, academies and the London Challenge. He was founding chair of the independent National Infrastructure Commission until he resigned to fight Brexit.

Windsor and Maidenhead

9580000110381

For Andrew, two Alices, Tom, Edmund and Sarah

'O brave new world,
That has such people in 't'

The authors' profits from this book will fund, as Europe awards, teenagers from disadvantaged families to study and work as volunteers within the European Union.

Contents

CONSIDERING that world peace can be safeguarded only by creative efforts commensurate with the dangers that threaten it ... RESOLVED to substitute for age-old rivalries ... a broader and deeper community among peoples long divided by bloody conflicts.

Preamble, European Coal and Steel
Community Treaty, 1951

RESTORING DIGNITY, REVIVING HOPE

Welcome sign, Birkenhead Food Bank, 2018

Brexit gives us a chance to finish the Thatcher revolution.

Nigel Lawson, *Financial Times*, 2 September 2016

Why is it that you, Sir Winston, became the champion for the European ideal? I believe this can be explained from two human qualities that also are the requisite qualities for statesmanship: greatness of thought, depth of feeling.

Konrad Adenauer to Winston Churchill, Presentation of
the International Charlemagne Prize, Aachen, 1956

Preface

This book was written in an intense collaboration between Christmas 2017 and Easter 2018, as Brexit started to unravel.

We had brilliant support. Philippe Schneider was our lead researcher and most penetrating critic. Charlie Atkins, Will Dry and Ethan Croft provided excellent assistance; they will go on to great things. For valuable insight we are grateful to Timothy Garton Ash, Anthony Barnett, Alan Bogg, Clive Efford, David Hopkin, Howard Goodall, Roger Liddle, Michael MacClay, Graham May, Pat Roche, Brendan Simms, Dennis Stevenson, Christopher Tyerman, Philip Waller, Barbara Want, Max Wind-Cowie and Alison Woollard. The fellows of Hertford College were hugely supportive – as was Jill Symons.

Our agent Caroline Michel and publisher Richard Beswick were outstanding. Richard's colleague Zoe Gullen piloted the book to publication. Steve Cox copy-edited rapidly, while Jane Acton devised our publicity.

Will would also like to thank Birgitte Andersen, CEO of

Big Innovation Centre (BIC) and member, along with Alex Edmans, Tom Gosling and Colin Mayer, of the steering group of the BIC's Purposeful Company Taskforce, which Will co-chairs with Clare Chapman. Their radical thinking on innovation and stakeholder capitalism is reflected here. Any misinterpretations are all our fault.

Roy Jenkins, Britain's only president of the European Commission and a great biographer of Winston Churchill, is our inspiration. His lesson to those who would make the weather: 'always argue to solutions, not to conclusions'. This book is about solutions. They are desperately needed.

AA and WH, St George's Day 2018

Saving Britain

Brexit voters were right. The status quo is insupportable. But the solution is not to leave the European Union. Our problems are made in Britain; they can only be solved in Britain. Europe does not impede this mission; it is indispensable.

We need to transform the way our country works. We need a new deal for a European Britain – more and better jobs, greater equality, high-quality public services, people of all backgrounds and localities treated with respect, given the opportunity and the power to thrive. To rupture our trade and our place in the world chasing economic moonbeams, to cower behind borders that shut out our continent and to seek to resurrect an unachievable island sovereignty – together, this is a dead end that can only result in widespread suffering.

Brexiters dodge these truths. Intent on creating 'Thatcherism in one country', they want us out of the EU at any cost. While feigning concern for the state of Britain, their real agenda, in the footsteps of Margaret Thatcher, is a small and feeble state, the imposition of austerity and unregulated markets. They want out of Europe because it stands in their way.

Two years after the referendum, the Brexiters' 'have cake and eat it' fantasies have evaporated. There is no Brexit dividend, rather the prospect of dismal economic growth and tax rises. The extra £350 million a week allegedly available for the NHS turns out not to exist once we have settled an exit bill of £39 billion and rising. Virtually no one still claims that we can retain the economic benefits of EU membership while leaving the European customs union and single market.

In a moment of truth, Theresa May conceded in March 2018 that the UK will have 'less market access' on leaving the EU – the first time in memory that a prime minister has made a reduction in British trade an avowed object of government policy. The prospect of 'quick and simple' trade deals outside the EU is now recognised as delusory, particularly with Trump's America and Xi's China; and the public is learning that the EU already has trade deals with more than sixty other countries, including Canada, Japan and South Korea – all in jeopardy on Brexit day. The global EU is the citadel of international free trade.

Brexiters were gleeful in the first months after the referendum that the economy appeared to be holding up, but Brexit was then way off. It was not even clear if it would ultimately happen. Two years on, with a firm Brexit date only months away, the economy is undermined. Growth has stalled and bad news intensifies. Inward investment into the UK has slumped £132 billion in the last year. Huge activity is being offshored. Britain is excluding itself from the Galileo European space project, damaging hopes to build a £40 billion space industry in the UK. The end of the EU Open Skies deal with the US is similarly grim for British airlines. The car industry fears its integration with European supply chains – critical to its success – is about to be severed. This story is repeated business sector by business sector. Britain has experienced currency, banking and fiscal crises since the war. Brexit, representing a crisis in our trading relationships and core growth model, is the gravest yet.

Still in the balance is an important debate about immigration, whose impact, along with austerity, was decisive in the Leave vote. Controlling immigrant inflows turns out to be more complex and difficult than many believed or asserted, given the scale of non-EU migration, the rights of more than a million British citizens who live in other EU countries and the economic needs of the country. Britain has done much better in integrating newcomers than Farage and the fear-mongers claim.

Equally worrying is the Brexit threat to European solidarity and democracy on which British security crucially depends. Europe is quivering before the rise of the populist right and an arc of ultra-nationalists extending from Serbia through Hungary and Poland to Putin's proto-fascist Russia. Democracy and the Enlightenment values that support it are in retreat. In the heart of Europe the rule of law is threatened by gangsterism and dangerous nationalist populism in the service of 'strong man' leaders. It was Churchill who said that Europe was where the weather comes from – and the winds have not changed.

Our vibrant links with Europe, to look out for each other in security and defence, to trade, to work, to travel, to do science and culture together, and so much else, are to be cut in return for isolation. At the same time we are courting new risks in Europe and at home. A hard border in Ireland is both dangerous and imminent. We are set to become a much diminished country. We are about to walk small.

This book, published only months before Britain is set to leave the EU in March 2019, aims to persuade fatalistic Remainers, and those Leave voters growing more and more uneasy, that there is a far better prospectus. Instead we can and should change Britain, and recommit to the EU.

The Brexit referendum was above all a clarion call from left-behind Britain that it will no longer tolerate being ignored and neglected. There needs to be a comprehensive response, and this book offers one. Many of those who voted Leave feel – rightly – that life in contemporary Britain is needlessly bleak, with too little chance of breaking out into anything better. They can see that the social contract is broken. Economic vitality in their local neighbourhoods is draining away. There is too little to be proud of and too much to be worried about. Politicians in Westminster are distant; people feel trapped and discarded.

The lie at the heart of Brexit is that this downward spiral can be stopped by leaving Europe. The answer lies rather in bold reform at home. Far from entrenching the Thatcherite revolution, with its permanent underclass and raging inequality, we must instead reverse it. Simultaneously we must adopt a thoroughly internationalist position abroad, one that protects our national interest and embraces our European destiny. Britain should lead, not leave; we should make, not break.

We start with an assessment of Brexit Britain: why it voted as it did, the conversion of the Conservative Party to an extreme mutation of Thatcherism – 'Faragism' – and the underlying truth that Brexit means domination *of* England by a self-serving 'wealth' elite and domination *by* England of Scotland, Ireland and Wales. It means handing the country over to the likes of Jacob Rees-Mogg, Boris Johnson and Nigel Farage, themselves exempt from the risks they propagate.

Shakespeare, Churchill, Newton, Keynes, Wollstonecraft, Darwin, Fawcett – animators of modern England – were all profoundly European in creed and ambition. The idea that we can be European while deserting Europe's institutions is fatuous; they are its practical embodiment. The alternative is isolation. When in 1938 Churchill rejected Chamberlain's misguided claim that the threat to Czechoslovakia, about to be subjugated by Hitler, was 'a quarrel in a faraway country between people of whom we know nothing', he spoke as powerfully against Brexit isolationism today as against the mistakes that paved the way for the Second World War. Our interdependencies are even greater today.

This book presents a vision of a European Britain which is the polar opposite of the Brexit dystopia. Facts and figures take us only so far. We appeal to the better angels and sinews of the English – a nation largely descended from European immigrants, including the Huguenot Farages – who are not isolationist, xenophobic and selfish. Our civilisation has been built on our capacity to assimilate and integrate other ideas, cultures and peoples. We must never stop.

At its best Britain is self-confident and open: relaxed, for example, that the top managers in the Premiership are all continental Europeans. Spaniard Rafa Benítez, when manager of Liverpool, was as passionate a campaigner for justice for the victims of Hillsborough as any Liverpudlian. The enthusiastic young audience at the Last Night of the Proms – a joyful celebration of European music – wave both the Union Jack and the EU flag. The quintessentially English composer Sir Edward Elgar dedicated the 'Nimrod' variation, played every Remembrance Sunday, to a German friend and mentor. Most of us are English, British and European. We want to welcome Europeans here, just as they welcome us in their countries.

Never in modern Britain has there been so much passionate Europeanism as since the Brexit referendum. The threat of losing Europe suddenly makes it valuable and urgent. In the European Union we make common cause in defence of values rooted in Christianity, democracy and geography. We want to share a continent where Europeans don't fight each other, don't prevent trade and travel, and where we allow our young men and women to live and work wherever they like. That's why there is a single market and a customs union. It's why there is a European Council, Commission, Parliament and Court, all freely established and supported by the elected parliaments of Europe. Europe is better for them.

These achievements have not been driven solely by an economic calculus: from the start they belonged to a bigger, nobler cause of representing European civilisation and values. This is why any form of Brexit is a mistake, including a so-called soft Brexit in which we struggle to retain a kind of association with Europe. It is a profound error to seek to leave Europe's free institutions. Never has Europe been so peaceful, democratic and prosperous as in the era of the European Union. Britain has been a huge beneficiary and made a huge contribution. We should not withdraw – now or ever.

We present a manifesto for a European Britain. It is critically important to end today's laissez-faire, sink-or-swim approach to economics and society, and instead to populate our hijacked capitalism with repurposed companies and employers which serve, not oppress, the people. We make the case for stakeholder capitalism. This should have been the agenda of New Labour; that the opportunity was passed up does not make it any less urgent today. New technology, especially the power of the internet and artificial intelligence, needs to be mobilised for the public good, while great institutions that serve the mass of people – like trade unions and building societies – must be reinvented for our time.

A new social contract should underwrite risk and opportunity, supported by a new willingness to invest public money where so desperately needed and to raise the necessary taxes fairly. Part of this social contract should be a far stronger notion of citizenship, including a national identity card system to assure citizens that we know exactly who is here and what they are entitled to. Today's huge digital companies – Google, Facebook, Amazon and Apple – should be made to serve the public good.

We propose a Great Charter for Modern Britain, a new Magna Carta eight hundred years after the founding document of English liberty, the first clause of which would hand power from Westminster to the cities, towns and counties of England.

The second clause would create a genuine federation of the United Kingdom, including a Senate to replace the House of Lords, located in the North of England, as champion of the rights and interests of the nations, cities and localities of the United Kingdom.

The Great Charter should be promulgated by the Queen in Parliament on 29 March 2019, the day the Brexiters intend to wrench Britain out of Europe. A Constitutional Convention should meet in the summer of 2019, perhaps in York, where Parliament met frequently after Magna Carta, to turn the Charter into a fully fledged written constitution, embodying radical devolution in England, an extension of the vote to sixteen- and seventeen-year-olds, and the social and economic rights which the British people have for too long been denied.

Both authors are proud British Europeans. Will learned that there is no Britain without Europe through his father, Captain William Hutton, who landed in Normandy on D-Day plus 2. Will writes:

After the battle of Caen, Dad was briefly asked to oversee hundreds of German prisoners of war. He told me that he looked at these young men, whose bravery in holding the city for some weeks against overwhelming odds he respected and who seemed indistinguishable from the young men he commanded – but caught up like his men in terrible events. He felt lucky that the accident of birth had meant he was not on the other side of the wire, and promised himself that he would do whatever necessary to prevent another European war. We Europeans shared common values, he insisted, embodied in the EU flag. On holidays in Europe throughout my childhood, if he met a German of the same age with a family he went out of his way to shake his hand in friendship – and my mother, brother and I followed his lead. He lived and died a British European.

Andrew is the son of Nicos Adonis, a Greek Cypriot who, in 1959, aged eighteen, travelled to London with his brothers and sisters, by boat and train via Venice, in search of a better life, escaping from the brutal war of independence with Britain then raging in Cyprus. Andrew writes:

My dad settled in London and had children while most of his siblings went back to Cyprus, only for them to return suddenly as refugees in 1974 after the Turkish invasion. Cyprus is still divided and Famagusta, where the Adonis family comes from, is still occupied by Turkey. For my family, England has been a refuge, a lifeline and – when not engaged in imperial atrocities – an inspiration. We are proud Londoners too. A European Union that Cyprus and Britain forge together is a pioneer of peace, prosperity and freedom.

Time is short. Since the referendum there has been an air of unreality. Is Britain really going to make itself meaner, smaller and poorer? The stuff of democracy is continual debate and discussion. It cannot be closed down. The people have the right to change Britain and stop Brexit. We urge just that.

1

Falling to pieces

Brexit has divided the country like little since the great battles over religion and the constitution in the sixteenth and seventeenth centuries. Britain is now in two mutually uncomprehending camps.

Above all, Brexit was a vote against an order that seems only to work for the educated and better off embracing broadly liberal and internationalist values. There were the majority of over-65s, certainly, looking back to a less liberal and more stable world, but for millions of others who voted Leave it was a cry of anger and despair.

Good jobs with good wages and prospects are increasingly rare. For many in modern Britain the social contract is broken. Vitality in their local neighbourhoods is ebbing away. There is too little to be proud of and too much to fear. Threats abound: new technologies, dead-end jobs, poor education, few decent apprenticeships, virtually no social mobility, career hopes disappearing, apparently unstoppable immigration, stagnating wages. Opportunity and the chance for self-improvement feel haphazard, reserved for privileged insiders and southerners. There is deep distrust of politicians and the government in remote London who have delivered these ills. Self-respect demands that they register their dissent and insist on a different settlement. They might end up worse off than today, but why not roll the dice for the chance of something better? Why stay trapped and ignored?

Mansfield versus Reading

Of Britain's sixty-three cities, Mansfield was the one with the highest percentage for Leave – 71 per cent – anywhere. For more than a generation this Nottinghamshire market city has been wrestling in vain to reinvent itself from its former dependence on mining and textiles. It is an urban island with an economy based on public services and retailing, no university, and with only a tiny private sector in knowledge-based activity. Well-paid jobs in companies with decent prospects are rare: average wages are 19 per cent below the national average, the employment rate is lower than average, and a huge number of its adults depend on benefits. Nearly a third of Mansfield's low-skill jobs are estimated to be at risk from automation and globalisation.

Reading, by contrast, voted 58 per cent Remain. The first stop out of Paddington on the InterCity 125s going west, the city is highly networked into London, Heathrow and the affluent Thames valley. Wages are 18 per cent above the national average; in 2016/17 welfare payments were £1100 lower on average for every resident living in Reading compared with

Mansfield. In Reading, with its university and about to get the Elizabeth Line straight into Central London, upward mobility is a lived reality. Why challenge a status quo that is working?

Too few Readings and too many Mansfields. This is the story of twenty-first-century urban England. Chatham, Doncaster, Corby, Stoke, Southend – and many more towns like them – took the opportunity to kick the economic and political establishment who for so long had neglected them. Appeals to stand by what we have in the European Union cut no ice. They did not feel part of Europe. Brussels and Berlin had dark ambitions to make British laws and to take British money, they felt. A tradition of imperial swagger stalks our culture and popular imagination, along with folk memories of two world wars. At games against German clubs, English football crowds still celebrate shooting down German bombers. To cap it all, we seemed to have lost control of our borders as immigrants flooded in unchecked, changing Britain fundamentally. Let's vote to leave – to get our country 'back'.

However, these are the symptoms not the causes of Brexit. The overriding reason is a Britain that has grown ruinously unequal. Education, living standards, health and the chance to express oneself through meaningful work – all have become a treacherous lottery. Not just between classes but geographically between regions, especially between North and South; and between thriving and failing towns and cities within the same region. Too many towns and cities contain large, barren wastelands.

Inequality in modern Britain is grotesque. Seven of the poorest ten regions in Northern Europe are in England.

All had substantial Brexit majorities. The richest region in Europe is Inner London. Astonishingly, regions in the North and Midlands as well as in Wales and Northern Ireland are between 5 per cent and 30 per cent poorer than West Virginia and Mississippi, two of the US's poorest and most economically challenged states. These regions are only 10–20 per cent better off than many of the regions in the former transition economies of the Czech Republic, Slovakia, Hungary and Slovenia and some regions in Portugal and Greece – bywords for economic backwardness. To drive the point home, levels of interregional inequality in the UK are 50 per cent higher than in similar-sized economies such as France and Germany, a third higher than Italy, and almost twice as high as Spain. The Brexit vote represented a popular revolt.

House prices, a national obsession, reflect this deformed pattern of wealth. In London they doubled between 2004 and 2016; they scarcely rose in Leave-voting Hartlepool, where comparable property costs 15 per cent of what it does in London. The twenty-seven areas of the country where property prices declined from 2004 to 2016 all voted Leave. Of the one hundred areas with the smallest increase in the price per habitable room (an index of property prices), ninety-three voted Leave. House prices have become a barometer of misery and entrapment. Where there is least demand to live, people voted Brexit.

Each person in London produces on average 75 per cent more than those in the North-East. The North-East has only a fraction as many private sector companies as the rich South-East. Again, these fissures are greater than found in other OECD countries, except for a few regions in Mexico and Canada made rich by oil and mining. The euro is often criticised for trying to stretch one currency over too much inequality: by that standard, sterling makes even less economic sense.

Remain-voting London benefits from its standing as a world city with a highly educated, nine million-strong population, larger than at any time in its history. Cities have always been flag-bearers of economic and social advance, fostering the myriad interactions that drive innovation and creativity, and then creating both demand for the resulting goods and services and the capacity to supply them.

But London has also been the beneficiary of a positive if undeclared industrial strategy: the build-up of financial services and creative industries springs from deliberate government policy. The same goes for infrastructure and transport. Though London makes up just 15 per cent of the population, it receives 35 per cent of the country's total infrastructure spending and 54 per cent of all transport infrastructure spending. Canary Wharf, now a massive financial centre, would not exist but for thirty years of huge state investment.

A parallel public investment in education has driven up educational standards; children from disadvantaged homes in London are twice as likely to go to university as their peers elsewhere in the country. Out of thirty-two London boroughs, twenty-nine are hotspots for social mobility as defined by the Social Mobility Commission. London has pioneered collaboration between the public and private sectors – whether the astonishing turnaround of London Docklands or the private-sector contributions made to the £16 billion Elizabeth Line.

In London, state industrial strategy, buoying up and triggering private-sector growth, has worked triumphantly.

The rest of England, with partial exceptions like Manchester and Bristol, has enjoyed no such public activism. There has been no parallel industrial strategy for English regions and left-behind towns, no parallel economic and social investment in them, and no institutional capacity to express local leadership. London's renaissance had not been exploited to regenerate the regions. They were supposed to boot-strap themselves into better economic and social outcomes by waving the wand of market forces. Even the Regional Development Agencies were abolished in 2010 by the Cameron government. Laissez-faire ruled, and turned out far more laissez than faire.

The Brexit vote shines a spotlight on how far Britain – especially England – has become economically and socially broken. Your life chances and quality of life depend on where you were born, and where you live. Place has ever more firmly become destiny. The referendum called time on it all.

Entrapment

In left-behind Britain social mobility has juddered to a halt, and this deals a double blow to people's attitudes. It drives social division deeper, while the sense that fate is set in stone makes the handicaps of birth, of race and where you live seem all the more toxic. It undermines self-respect.

The Social Mobility Commission's 2017 Report – the last with former Labour minister Alan Milburn as chair – put it bluntly: 'There is a fracture line running deep through our labour and housing markets and our education system. Those on the wrong side of this divide are losing out and falling behind.'

Again the statistics are stark. In Westminster, 63 per cent of children disadvantaged enough to be eligible for free school meals achieve A* to C in English and Maths GCSE; on the Isle of Wight only 27 per cent do. In Kensington and Chelsea, 50 per cent of disadvantaged pupils make it to university; in Hastings, Barnsley and Eastbourne, a mere 10 per cent do. In these social-mobility 'coldspots' there is virtually nothing available for those who do not make it to university: for example, a quarter of young people in Yorkshire's South Ribble are not in education, training or employment. Not one former industrial area of the Midlands or the North has bucked the trend by becoming a hotspot for social mobility – indeed 23 per cent of them rank as coldspots. The thirty regions the Social Mobility Commission identified as the worst coldspots for social mobility, ranging from Weymouth to Carlisle, all voted Leave. Twenty-one embraced Brexit by 60 per cent or more.

Part of this crisis is caused by austerity and too little public investment. In 2016/17 London spent about £1000 more per pupil in local authority-maintained schools than the South-West and East Midlands could afford – the regions with the lowest attainment scores for disadvantaged pupils. Coastal Britain is particularly hard hit: it has proportionally more unqualified secondary teachers than the least deprived inland areas. All these facts are of long standing, but little has been done to address them. Chair Alan Milburn and Deputy Chair Gillian Shephard (a former Conservative education secretary), despairing at the government's lack of drive, resigned in December 2017.

Disadvantage is heaped on disadvantage. Those who live in these condemned areas suffer a health crisis too. The numbers make you reel. There was a 165 per cent rise in the prescribing of antidepressant drugs in England between 1998 and 2012, with disproportionate rises in the ex-industrial towns of the North. In Blackpool, 331 per 1000 people were prescribed antidepressants in 2012/13 – one-third of the whole population, and five times higher than in the prosperous London borough of Brent. The now routine prescription of antidepressants is for what local GPs diagnose as 'shit life syndrome'. Deaths from liver disease alone – caused by alcohol abuse and obesity – are eight times higher per 100,000 in Blackpool than in South Norfolk.

The disadvantaged, like the better-off, only have so much mental bandwidth: their minds are dominated by a struggle to get by each day – to get to the next meal, to find the cash for the next bus ride and to pay for heat, light and shelter. For example, half the country practically never visit the dentist: sales of £10 DIY dental kits, self-administering dental treatment, are booming. There is just not the mental space to gather themselves to escape from their entrapment.

In consequence, in many parts of left-behind Britain life expectancy is stagnating and even declining. The life expectancy for Blackpool is 74.3 years, for Knowsley 76.8 years; for affluent East Dorset it is 82.8 years. Leave voters did not know the figures, but they could certainly feel the social facts they represented.

The impact is like a fast-metastasising cancer. Geographic and social isolation become self-reinforcing. As people with job prospects leave property becomes cheaper, so attracting in people who for whatever reason are struggling. The neighbourhoods become locked into a spiral of poverty and marginalisation. This is what is happening to Blackpool, Hartlepool and Grimsby.

It is part of a new and dangerous process of segregation. Knowledge-based economic activity is increasingly clustering in London and the major cities, with a parallel process of attracting human capital, attendant rise in property prices and a virtuous circle of growth begetting growth – the mirror image of the downward spiral. Worse, the housing market operates to seal areas off. In declining neighbourhoods, only the exceptionally able and ambitious escape.

Left-behind Britain

The figures above will shock most readers, but that too is a crucial part of the Brexit rupture. Mutual understanding has broken down between left-behind Britain and decision-makers and opinion-formers based mostly in London.

The social commentator David Goodhart has called this a 'great divide' between 'Anywheres' and 'Somewheres'. The Anywheres, he writes, 'have portable "achieved" identities, based on educational and career success which makes them comfortable and confident with new places and people'. On the other side are people rooted inescapably in their geo-graphical identity. These are the Somewheres. 'They have lost economically with the decline of well-paid jobs for people without qualifications and culturally, too, with the disappear-ance of a distinct working-class culture and the marginalisation of their views in the public conversation.'

This portrayal of a divide is too stark. There is a balance to be struck: pride in place coexists for most of us with a willingness to be open. Thus football fans will be loyal to their local team and chant insults at visiting fans as a demon-stration of their pride in place, but few fans, even committed Somewheres, are so insular that they want no foreign players or foreign managers. Yet Goodhart captures a truth. His classi-fication helps explain a Britain that is growing more and more segregated.

The country has not been good at navigating these cross-currents – or even understanding them. Our broad elite has been uninformed and uncomprehending to the point of indif-ference about the sentiments of the Somewheres. There are remnants of public service and concern for the commonweal amongst the public-spirited professional classes who step up to be teachers, doctors, school governors and charity trustees, but they are the minority. The generation of officers who served in two world wars, sharing in the misery and trials of combat, has died. Their men knew that their leaders were going through the same experience; the officer class in turn felt an obligation to deliver the common good – personified by politicians like Harold Macmillan, Ted Heath and Denis Healey, and their counterparts in post-war boardrooms and the officers' mess.

They were men of responsibility, service and duty. Their successors never served in the same way. Moreover, many chose and choose to educate their children in the costly and rarefied atmosphere of exclusive private schools.

Whatever their virtues as educational establishments, England's private schools neither accept nor inculcate much sense of civic obligation. It is not in their DNA. The elite that has emerged is trained and feels entitled to manage and govern; it is not taught to sacrifice or contribute to the common good. Repeated attempts to persuade private schools to collaborate more than tokenistically with state schools have flopped. 'The nature and convertibility of the new elites,' writes the political theorist Ivan Krastev, 'makes them practically independent of their own nations. They are not dependent on their country's education system or the National Health Service. They have lost the ability to share the passions of their communities.'

The Remain elite rarely engaged with the visceral concerns of their white, Brexit 'cut-immigration' fellow citizens. By contrast, Farage and the leaders of the Leave campaign had the wit to pay lip-service to white working-class concerns; indeed it was a brilliant camouflage for their 'Thatcherism in one country' ideology. It became good sport to tease people from the same social background as elitist, in the same breath as making knowingly false claims about the ease of striking trade deals, or diverting a mythical £350 million a week to the NHS, confident they will never be held to account. Or if they are, they just laugh it off – 'the rough and tumble of politics' – an insouciance that has cost the country dear.

In parallel the business elite has redefined its obligations solely in terms of the economic interests of the firm, and in particular of directors and shareholders. Company leaders in the aftermath of the Second World War understood that the companies they led had a social dimension: they established defined-benefit pension funds, recognised and negotiated with trade unions, albeit uneasily, and enlisted in organisations like the Industrial Society, founded in 1918 to promote the welfare, education and skills of working-class men and women. All that now belongs to another universe.

UK business, following the American lead in the 1980s, has declared that its objective is to maximise short-term shareholder value, and in the process our business leadership has become detached from wider society. Executive pay has become so extravagant that Sir Richard Lambert, former director-general of the CBI and ex-editor of the *Financial Times*, has warned against the risk of top executives being viewed as 'aliens'. Shareholders badger their boards to do everything in their power to deliver short-term profits, under threat of jumping ship. All relationships – with place, with workers, with supply chains, with shareholders and with customers – are seen as contingent upon the supreme objective of driving the share price higher and faster. Vast executive bonuses turn upon this. Employees are increasingly perceived as costs to be minimised, along with troublesome overheads like pensions. British capitalism has taken on a harsher, callous hue – but without even the compensating benefits of rising productivity and growth.

The collapse of the construction company Carillion – tellingly the only major company headquartered in the city of Wolverhampton, the heart of Leave-voting England – was a salutary tale. Its board put the payment of large dividends before proper contributions to the pension fund, which it self-servingly deferred. Carillion's failure is part of a wider story of corporate mishaps and debacles linked with collusive accountancy. The litany extends from the banks, through firms like Tesco and BT with their financial irregularities, to the bribery cases that have so damaged the reputation of Rolls-Royce, BAE Systems and GlaxoSmithKline (GSK). The public service delivery industry suffers similarly. Outsourcing companies Serco and G4S have had to repay £180 million for their shameless overcharging on tagged prison offenders. Learndirect, privatised and sold to the private equity arm of Lloyds Bank in 2011 and until recently Britain's biggest training provider, proved not to be training tens of thousands of its apprentices.

These inadequate companies have stapled themselves into the warp and woof of day-to-day life. Switch on the light, catch the bus, post a letter, turn off the oven, drink a glass of water, register for an apprenticeship, use a train, be sent to prison, park the car or eat the food in the hospital canteen – it's all provided by private companies. The amount of activity now performed by organisations we all own and whose overriding purpose is public service is minimal. It used to be a pride of our society that institutions like the National Grid, the Royal Mail or British Gas were run by executives who ultimately had to put the public's interest first: it is a bond severed. No one is now watching our back.

Nor is the notion of service noticeable in the wider business community. Whether tax havens or tax evasion, zero-hours contracts or poverty wages, or the mega-levels of directors' pay, the message is the same. All that matters is the bottom line and high reward for those at the top. British voters' trust in business has plummeted. Too few leading British companies and business leaders saw it as their role to speak out for the pro-EU case in the referendum: the prior obligation was to a narrowly defined view of their business, which they feared they might upset by being 'political'. But by then it was too late. Few voters would have trusted them as speaking for a wider British public interest in any case. The pass had been sold.

Left to rot

The UK's problems have deep roots. British industrialisation happened spontaneously and we mistook first-mover advantage for natural and enduring gains. We failed to build the industrial, educational and financial institutions to match those of our fast-advancing rivals in North America and Northern Europe.

By the turn of the twentieth century the UK's share of global industrial output was already in steep decline. Narrow patterns of specialisation, especially in staple goods like cotton, left many areas vulnerable to competition from more efficient producers. At its height more than half of British exports were textiles. But it was an industry not underpinned by a skills and financial system; nor were its firms owned for the long term. Amazingly, even in the late 1940s the

Lancashire industry depended heavily on spinning mules, and through the 1950s on power-looms, even as cotton textile industries around the world were adopting much more modern ring spinning and automatic looms.

The North of England's cities and towns were heavily dependent on similarly specialised single industries without an adequate training, scientific or financial system to underpin them. They lacked the civic and business leadership and the institutions to restructure themselves. Worse, the prevailing laissez-faire doctrine was that industrial restructuring would happen spontaneously in response to market forces. Over the twentieth century, whether the pottery towns of Staffordshire, mining villages of South Yorkshire, mill towns either side of the Pennines, specialist steel towns around Sheffield, or ship-building on Tyneside – all were left to fend for themselves in a cold climate.

There was a period between 1931 and 1950 when the industrial Midlands and North relaunched themselves, thanks to the industrial activism and state direction of the financial system that was triggered after the Great Recession and boosted by the Second World War. The Bank of England, apart from pegging the bank rate at 2 per cent, which would last for nearly twenty years, forced Britain's banks to reorganise and then to supply long-term cheap loans to the cotton, shipbuilding and steel industries. A cluster of new companies embodying the then frontier technologies – ICI, Hawker Siddeley, Thorn, Austin-Morris – emerged, backed by the Bankers Industrial Development Corporation and government grants, which were to underpin the triumphant feats of production during the war, when 'all in this together' meant what it said. Through the 1940s the same alchemy of state-led innovation and state direction of credit drove Britain to global leadership in innovations including radar, artificial rubber, nylon, magnetron valves, early computers and jet engines – and was sustained by Attlee's Labour government as exports boomed in the post-war years. These two decades are Britain's unsung years of economic success, winning us a world war, out-producing Germany, transforming British society and by 1950 giving us – well-known flaws aside – one of the most modern economies in the industrialised world. For a brief period Britain stumbled on the alchemy of successful capitalism.

The industrial superiority was not to survive. In part, British dominance was inevitably challenged, first by the reconstructed economic powers in Europe and then latterly by the newly industrialising economies of Asia. But the Conservative Party's growing repudiation of all forms of public intervention, ownership and strategy – and Labour's weaknesses in developing these tools – led to the ever-closer embrace of financial liberalisation, deregulation and the reining back of the alleged incubus of the state as the state's own default economic strategy. There was too little intellectual or political interest in creating a publicly led ecosystem, embracing scientific research, education and supportive business/finance relationships, that would foster economic growth: the division was between advocates of forms of state intervention as steps towards socialism and on the other hand the free market.

The epoch-framing election of Margaret Thatcher in 1979 set the parameters for all her successors. Her intellectual and political dominance was so strong that the governments that came after were essentially 'standstill' administrations. Major and Cameron advanced Thatcherism a bit: Blair and Brown mitigated it a bit, but no determined or sustained effort was made by any of them to modernise the economies of old industrial Britain or challenge her free-market paradigm. Perhaps the most egregious examples are the still devastated former mining communities, more than thirty years on from the miners' strike, left literally to crumble. But many of the smaller towns and cities whose economies were based on one now-defunct industry are scarcely better off. All voted Leave in 2016.

The doctrine that 'the market' must rule has led to profound territorial and income inequalities. What Britain requires is the polar opposite. All successful capitalisms owe their dynamism to the interplay and interdependence between public and private, as Britain learned both from the achievements of 1931–50 and from the more recent experience of the successful London economy. Capitalism has to be primed to work for the mass of people, together with a functioning social contract, or else it doesn't work at all. It must not serve a tiny minority.

Will Hutton made the case for stakeholder capitalism in *The State We're In*, published in January 1995. In a speech in Singapore a year later Tony Blair seemed to endorse it. But New Labour did not want to take on either the business elite or the Murdoch media. It wrongly believed that Thatcherism had cured the ills of the British economy. Stakeholder capitalism never took off, and New Labour chose the path of least resistance – mitigating the Thatcherite settlement but not challenging it. It was one of three strategic errors, alongside the war in Iraq and Blair's timidity on Europe, that would define the New Labour years, and is one of the principal explanations of Brexit. It is not enough to mitigate laissez-faire. It needs to be ended.

Austerity and the collapse of the Thatcherite growth model

On Friday 10 October 2008 Britain's then-largest bank, the Royal Bank of Scotland, came within hours of collapse. Only a trillion-pound bailout saved it and the rest of the British financial system from the domino impact of a series of bank failures that would have triggered a nationwide economic slump as the flow of credit imploded. Even as it was, Britain suffered its biggest-ever post-war recession and slowest-ever recovery. Public spending as a share of a shrunken economy climbed to nearly 50 per cent of GDP, while the public deficit on the same measure topped 10 per cent. The repercussions have shaped the British economy and society for the last decade, and snowball to this day.

For the financial crisis was the natural culmination of the low-saving, high-consumption growth model propelled by limitless credit that the UK had developed out of the triumphalist Thatcherite deregulation of banks and building societies in the 1980s, but which had left the basic weaknesses of the economy unaddressed, ranging from the skills system to the endemic disconnect between finance and business. As the tide of credit ebbed after the crisis, the poverty of the former deregulated growth model was more and more exposed. Suddenly the UK had to look to underlying productivity growth to fuel the growth of real wages that underpins citizens' prosperity. But it did not have the means. Apart from a small knot of high-performing companies in specialised parts of manufacturing (like pharmaceuticals) and privileged services such as magic-circle law firms and the big four accountancy firms, the UK's reliance on a long tail of mediocre and downright underperforming companies devoid of structures to change or support them was cruelly exposed. Nor was there a system to boost innovation-rich companies to scale up quickly. Productivity growth has stubbornly stagnated or hardly grown at all: it is now 17 per cent below where it could have expected to be had the pre-crisis trends continued.

Companies have survived by unloading risk onto the shoulders of ordinary workers. They have deliberately moved away from standardised contracts with proper employment rights – holiday and sickness pay, pension, union recognition, paternity and maternity benefits – and instead designated workers as imaginarily self-employed, disposable contractors responsible for all such costly employment benefits themselves. At the extreme is the employment twilight zone of zero-hours contracts. As a result the UK's record in job generation looks impressive in raw figures – the unemployment rate has halved over the last seven years – but quality of jobs, work and living standards have deteriorated year by year.

The 7 per cent fall in real wages – wages adjusted for inflation – since 2008 is the biggest and longest on record, and the worst, alongside Greece, among the leading industrialised countries. In 2015 around 20 per cent of jobs in the UK were paid less than the voluntary living wage of just £7.85 an hour.

The gig economy of casualised work without benefits has replaced full employment. Permanent jobs have been replaced by transient contractualised work – a growing pool of the unskilled. Eight hundred thousand workers are officially on zero-hours contracts, with one hundred thousand more added every year. As many as 15 per cent of workers are classed as self-employed – a proportion that has doubled in a generation. Half of those returning to employment after the 2008 crash went back to part-time jobs or self-employment. Low-skilled jobs, or 'elementary occupations', which were relatively few in number even as recently as the 1990s (in 1993, just 7 per cent of young women worked in low-skilled jobs, and 14 per cent of young men), have risen: 21 per cent of young women and 25 per cent of young men now work in low-skilled rudimentary 'elementary' jobs. The result is that millions of those in work – in addition to those out of work and on benefits – are living hand to mouth.

A third of Britain's workforce was in poverty for at least one year between 2012 and 2015, with 4.6 million locked in a state of persistent poverty. Borrowing is essential to making ends meet. Household debt is soaring towards the levels in the years just before the financial crisis. The saving rate has fallen to its lowest level since 1963, when records began.

Brutalising this inequality, those living hard-pressed lives have witnessed the immense rewards accruing to the richest. The top 1 per cent have more than doubled their share of income over the last thirty-five years to 8.6 per cent. There is one rule for the vastly better off, another for the growing mass of the rest. Tellingly, out of the ten local authorities where workers receive the lowest wages in the country, eight voted Leave.

Superimposed upon all of this was one of the most aggressive assaults on public spending ever mounted by a Western democracy. George Osborne, a Thatcherite chancellor with some Blairite flourishes, chose not to deploy a mix of tax increases and spending cuts to lower the very high public sector deficit: instead, virtually the entire burden was placed on reducing what he and Cameron characterised as New Labour's bloated public sector. Public spending and borrowing were depicted as moral vices; public servants despised as quasi-parasites. Private spending was a virtue, taxation a morally deplorable confiscation of private assets.

On average, as estimated by the independent Office for Budget Responsibility (OBR), per capita spending on public services will have fallen 23 per cent between 2007/8 and 2018/19. The cuts beyond health, education and defence – all of which have suffered despite the alleged protection they were offered – are close to incredible. Spending on the criminal justice system and local government will have fallen cumulatively by over 30 and 40 per cent respectively, causing not just hardship but the implosion of Britain's prisons and care system. In early 2018 a succession of local authorities, including Conservative-run Surrey and Northamptonshire, froze new spending to meet their minimum statutory obligations. Northamptonshire imposed emergency spending cuts to avoid an illegal deficit. In many parts of the country the bins are now emptied only once every three weeks, and rubbish is piled up in the streets, attracting rats and foxes. The NHS experienced in early 2018 its worst-ever winter crisis, with warnings that it could not continue to sustain a universal health service.

Food banks, described as the fourth emergency service by their managers in Birkenhead (see chapter 3), have become a proxy for the combined effect of austerity hitting public services and the decline of good jobs. 2016 was the ninth successive year in which food-bank demand increased. No wonder the idea blazoned on the Leave bus of recovering an easy £350 million a week for the NHS from the EU seemed so attractive: in one mighty bound voters could protect and invest in a core public service. A poisonous cocktail of deindustriali-sation, the financial crisis and the ideological assault on public services came together in the Brexit vote. The genius of the Eurosceptic right was to take none of the blame for its own domestic policies, but to offload it instead onto the EU and immigration.

Immigration as bogey

Nigel Farage's technique, as we describe in the next chapter, was to make the foreigner the scapegoat for Britain's home-grown crisis. It is the age-old trick of hard-right populists; in Britain it comes straight out of the playbook of Enoch Powell and Sir Oswald Mosley. It was aided and abetted by the coalition government which through austerity needlessly intensified the lived experience of crisis and poverty.

Blame all your ills, Farage told the white working class, not on the protracted failure to engage with Britain's deep economic and structural failures, but on immigrants and the political leaders who let them in. He relentlessly assailed the liberal pro-European 'establishment' – New Labour and Cameron Conservative alike – for not wanting to talk about the sudden development of mass immigration after the fateful 2004 decision to admit East Europeans without even a transition period, while rarely if ever overstepping the line into outright racism. The EU and Islamic terrorism entered the Brexit blender and came out as a single stream of threats from outside our borders to the English way of life. Farage ventured where at the time only a few of the Eurosceptic right dared to tread, while the Conservative Party stayed silent on immigration. Without the orchestrated focus on the 'other' as a cause of the British crisis, the referendum would never have been won.

Of course there are EU immigration hotspots – parts of Lincolnshire and South Yorkshire for example – where the indigenous population feels strongly that they are under threat. Nothing was done to stem the tide of indignation. For all its alleged liberalism, the Cameron government did not dare to voice the economic case for immigration, or insist that Britain had assimilated waves of immigrants before while staying no less British, or that the British reciprocally could go and work in the EU. It failed to distinguish student immigrants from worker immigrants, or to tackle the special pressures on those local areas where immigration was high. It might not have turned the tide, but some of the sting could have been drawn. Cameron also foolishly scrapped the Blair/Brown scheme for a national system of ID cards, so that public authorities would know who was in the country legally with a right to work – a badge of citizenship (and of control) that the rest of Europe uses readily.

The rapid rise in immigration, a hot issue in any country, was simply allowed to fester, with fears inflamed by a frenzied right-wing media. Such was the scale of media lies that polls report that people think that the level of EU immigration is three times higher than it truly is. Seventy-three per cent of those who voted Leave were anxious about that pseudo-tsunami.

Democracies can only function if citizens have accurate and true information – particularly on something as emotive as immigration. That did not happen. The economic 'facts' propagated by Leave and its media are just wrong, usually by taking one scandal and pumping it up into a false example of a general trend. EU migrants from Eastern Europe come to Britain to work. They are young and educated by their host countries, who criticise their exodus as a brain drain from which Britain ruthlessly benefits. Because they are young, they work, and they hardly make use of the health, education and welfare services; they contribute billions more to the Exchequer in taxes than they take out. One estimate is that immigrants from Eastern Europe contributed a net £15 billion between 2001 and 2011. It was an unknown and unproclaimed fact. With an ageing population, Britain needs its immigrants.

Any downward impact on wages, to the extent that it can be identified, is small and localised. The Bank of England, for example, finds that all EU immigration between 2004 and 2011 reduced semi/unskilled services-sector wages by less than 1 per cent – tantamount to a reduction in annual pay rises of about a penny an hour given average wages in the sector. Of course 1 per cent, even over eight years, is not negligible; but neither is it large, especially as minimum wages rose by 4 per cent over the same period. It is certainly not worth rupturing all our major trade relations for, imposing much bigger losses. Other research confirms these findings, with small wage losses for those in the bottom 10 per cent of the pay distribution but offset by wage gains for those in the middle of the pay ladder. This reflects the fact that immigrants add not only to labour supply, but also to its demand: they earn money and spend it on goods and services, pushing up wages in other parts of the economy.

There are some blackspots where unscrupulous employers in the black economy use exploited EU immigrants to under-cut wages and standards, but in overall terms their impact is small. It is not immigrants who have caused the drop in real wages; it is lack of productivity. There have been pressures on Britain's infrastructure, notably in housing, and in public services – but they were intensified by indiscriminate spend-ing cuts. For example, to blame housing shortages and soaring house prices on immigrants is to miss the mark. Britain's hous-ing crisis is again a crisis of our own making, an interaction of the way we restrictively plan, under-tax, under-build and over-supply housing finance. It may have been exacerbated at the margin by immigration, but it was certainly not caused by it.

The wider story is that immigration, providing we hold it at manageable levels, is a source of general benefit. EU immi-grants' contribution to the NHS, for example, has become ever more obvious as the inflow of trained nurses and doctors from the EU has slowed down post Brexit referendum: nurses from the EU applying to work in Britain fell from ten thousand to one thousand between September 2016 and September 2017. As the *Lancet* comments, the impact of Brexit on the health service will 'range from somewhat negative to very negative, with few opportunities'. EU scientific researchers in our universities, drivers of taxis, cleaners of our offices, starters of businesses and restaurants and managers in our workplaces have all enriched Britain.

For all this, the central truth is that after 2004 immigration took off at levels unknown for a generation, and the spike proved explosive. Politicians appeared to have lost control, and to some extent they did – with causes and consequences discussed in later chapters. In this context the economic benefits could have been better explained, fired by the conviction that Britain shapes its migrants rather than migrants shaping Britain. It was a road not taken, opening the way to the disaster of Brexit. We cannot continue to downplay either the benefits of immigration or the issues it raises. It is time for the truth.

The EU takes the edge off

Liberal Britain's biggest failure was not to argue passionately and consistently for the worth of Britain's EU membership – whether financial, political, economic or cultural. The benefits were taken for granted: greater economic growth, the EU's free-trade agreements with over sixty other countries covering over half of British exports, the avalanche of transformative inward investment, the heft that membership has given to

British foreign and security policy over many years (a mutual benefit), EU institutions that invested in left-behind Britain in a way that Whitehall had never done, along with a host of initiatives that promoted better work and a better environment across our continent. Instead, progressive Britain connived in the softer option – indulging the undertow of sniping against the EU at every level from the geometry of fruit and veg to dreams of ever closer union, while rarely arguing for its benefits. In June 2016 the whirlwind was reaped.

Brexiters want to torch all these benefits – for what? To address the problems outlined in this chapter? Hardly. As Nigel Lawson, high priest of Thatcherism, Brexit and climate-change denial, has declared, the aim is to complete the Thatcherite 'revolution' of permanent austerity for the poor and welfare for the rich, to sum up Thatcherism and its continued legacy in the economic and social sphere.

The first loss is economic. In 2017 there has been a world boom with nearly every country growing faster than normal. There is one telling exception, Britain, whose subnormal growth of around 1.4 per cent per year is projected by the Office for Budget Responsibility to drag on for the next five years. (Here the only dissenters are the discredited 'Economists for Brexit' whose ambitious growth forecasts have already been proven wrong.) Without the global boom, and especially the strong growth in the EU over the last two years, Britain would have struggled even more than it has done. The young can barely afford to rent or buy houses – by 2025 only 10 per cent of under-35s can expect to own their own home. Household savings have collapsed, while household debt has been rising as people borrow to sustain their spending – the longest period this has happened on record, and one of the reasons that the economically depressive effect of Brexit has not been more acute. The rise in investment during an economic upturn is the shallowest for more than half a century, so the Bank of England estimates. Uncertainty and unease haunt the economy. Can Britain really do better outside the EU than it did inside it? The EU was taking the edge off our lamentable economic and social performance. No longer.

Governor of the Bank of England Mark Carney says that Brexit cost Britain £10 billion in lost output in 2017, costs that he believes are likely to grow. The *Financial Times* reckons the shortfall was nearer £18 billion in 2017, or just under £350 million a week – the figure that the Leave campaign promised to take back. Moreover a cluster of reports – from the Scottish government, the mayor of London, and leaked central government papers assessing the long-term economic impact of Brexit – all judge that the outlook is one of lower output and growth than otherwise would have been the case. By the saddest of ironies, Leave-voting British regions, much more proportionally hooked into doing business with the EU, are now set to take a disproportionate hit as compared with London and the South East, whose economy is more oriented to global services and has held up better.

EU trade arrangements cover 54 per cent of our exports, directly to EU countries and indirectly to more than sixty others. The Brexiter contention – a prophecy examined in more critical detail in chapter 6 – is that Britain can quickly reproduce those arrangements and strike better deals for the balance of our exports not covered, even though our competitive advantage is in services on which it is notoriously difficult if not impossible to achieve free-trade agreements. That claim is gormless moonshine. In the real world there is no queue of fairy godmothers waiting to grant free favours. Trade with the Commonwealth would have to quintuple to compensate for what we are losing in Europe: it simply is not going to happen. Within the EU the UK has held back accelerating deindustrialisation by linking our producers into multiple high-value just-in-time manufacturing supply chains across the continent. Seventy per cent of British manufactured exports, largely to Europe, are in intermediate and capital goods contributing to other producers' supply chains – not final consumer goods.

Likewise, UK production is dependent on imports from the EU. It is well advertised that the UK car industry is enjoying a resurgence. Less well known is that on average only 41 per cent of their content is UK-produced – 59 per cent is overseas content, of which two-thirds comes from the EU. Comparing the British economy with a control group of similar economies that did not join the EU, economists estimate that had Britain stayed out of the EU over the last forty years, its per capita incomes would have been some 24 per cent lower. The combination of more intensive competition inside the EU, an inability to bend British policy to protect economic laggards, and higher rates of inward investment have promoted economic growth and living standards. This greater prosperity and other beneficial effects will unravel when – if – Britain leaves the single market and customs union.

For over the last forty years, cumulatively a trillion pounds of inward investment has been made in Britain. Some of this was because of British openness, our flexible labour markets and the English language. But a significant proportion, especially from Japan, was because of our access to European markets – the so-called 'aircraft-carrier' effect – which in left-behind regions like the North-East offset the disastrously low rate of indigenous UK investment. Think the Nissan plant in Sunderland. Approaching five hundred multinationals have their regional or global headquarters in Britain for the same reason, bringing precious jobs in business services – ranging from advertising to IT – that follow headquarters. They are now reassessing their commitment. At best they are freezing further investment in Britain: at worst they are packing their bags.

There will be sweeping negative effects on public investment. The EU has been a reliable and consistent investor in left-behind parts of the country including Wales and the South-West, which have a per capita GDP of less than 75 per cent of the EU average. For them the EU's Regional Development Fund (ERDF) investments have been a lifeline. Wales and the Valleys will cumulatively receive just over £1.8 billion between 2014 and 2020. In Wales alone, since 2007 the European Regional Development Fund has created 36,640 new jobs and 11,900 new businesses. There are eleven UK regions, mainly in the Midlands and North of England, that qualify for investment because their per capita GDP is between 75 and 90 per cent of the EU average. In the North the ERDF can claim 70,546 jobs and 18,128 new businesses to its credit since 2007. With the scrapping of the Regional

Development Agencies, the ERDF is one of the few pillars remaining of an activist regional policy.

Nor is it alone. The European Investment Bank's (EIB) lending had grown to reach £6 billion in the twelve months before the referendum result – within sight of Britain's EU net budgetary contribution – and was an important source of finance for Britain's many high-tech start-ups and crucial infrastructure projects, especially outside London. For example, the EIB supported the installation of fifty-three million smart meters by 2020, with seven million already installed in the EIB's largest strategic project. But since Article 50 was triggered in March 2017 lending collapsed to £377 million for the remaining nine months of 2017. It is a massive gap to fill. Apart from the fledgling British Business Bank, Britain has no institutional capacity to replace this lost financing: already it is having a freezing effect on the financing of start-ups, especially outside London.

So the palsy of Brexit spreads. The NHS not only depends on doctors and nurses from across the EU, their numbers now declining sharply; it is part of an EU-wide health system that shares knowledge, vaccines, skills, drug licensing and researchers without which its capacity to do its job is threatened. Agricultural incomes are likely to fall outside the EU and there will be greater uncertainty as food supplies, particularly the supply of fresh food from the EU, cannot be readily or cheaply replaced. In the next phase of EU research funding between 2020 and 2027, Britain would have expected to be a major net beneficiary because our research universities are both outstanding and excellent at collaborative research with

European universities. The UK has consistently led more EU-related health projects than any other country, ranging from cancer to digital healthcare. EU researchers can enter and leave the UK freely, along with their families. No more if we Brexit. The curtain is falling on all those gains. The impact on Britain's science base can only be corrosive.

The upside, claim the Thatcherite-Brexiters, is that Britain will be 'unshackled' from a 'corpse' of EU regulation. This is Alice in Wonderland. Within the EU the UK already has one of the most lightly regulated economies in the industrialised world, only marginally less so than the famously lightly regulated US. Moreover, the evidence from the 'balance of competences' review (commissioned by David Cameron in 2013 and which we discuss in detail in chapter 2) was that the EU was not interfering excessively in any aspect of British life, not least because recent EU initiatives such as Regulatory Fitness and Performance (REFIT) have had the explicit aim of simplifying EU regulation and reducing its burden. Indeed, if anything, Britain has been gold-plating EU legislation knowing full well that such reinforcement is what British consumers want. In any case much of the regulation, as we argue in chapter 6, is done in order to create a level playing field and promote competition and trade. Exporters from now on face trade frictions that will redouble 'red tape' and ratchet up business costs. As none of this fits the Brexiters' agenda, instead they just parrot the mantra that the EU delivers a sackful of regulation.

On Planet Brexit, regulation has to be bad, so if they have their way with abolition most British workers and citizens – the beneficiaries – will quickly feel the loss. Most 'red tape' exists to foster a greener environment, diminish climate change and promote good working conditions – all of which command strong support in the UK. The EU has secured rights across the board: health and safety protection, parity for part-time and agency workers, access to paid annual holidays, and parental leave, to name just a few. The Working Time Directive is a particular bête noire for the Brexit right. Yet it has resulted in seven hundred thousand fewer employees working more than forty-eight-hour weeks compared with 1998. It won for six million workers – mainly women in low-paid jobs – the right to paid annual leave. As the TUC declares: 'This amounts to a significant financial transfer from employers to predominantly low-paid women workers.' It also allows parents to take time off work in the case of a family emergency – a right that a quarter of working parents exercise each year.

The EU has also greatly improved health and safety at the workplace: forty-one out of the sixty-five new health and safety regulations introduced between 1997 and 2009 originated in the EU. The EU, for instance, required the UK to improve its regulations on the lethal risks from asbestos. Again, it has a much better record for protecting those in need than the UK government. Large employers, with over one thousand employees domestically or at least 150 in two European countries, must set up a European Work Council to consult and inform employees of plans and projects. An employer planning collective redundancies must consult the workers with specific information. The EU has also determined that the bonuses of bankers cannot amount to more than their yearly salary without shareholder approval. These are the regulations from which Lord Lawson, 'taking back control', wants to escape.

The other key source of the EU's allegedly suffocating legislation is environmental protection. It has been a leading advocate of international measures to contain the growth of greenhouse gases. The EU Emissions Trading Scheme, covering more than eleven thousand installations, is the world's most ambitious effort to create an emissions trading scheme that caps the level of emissions from the burning of fossil fuels. Recent reforms have gone some way to stabilising the price of carbon permits which had hitherto been a weakness of the scheme, further strengthening incentives for companies to reduce their carbon footprint. The EU has also used its significant trade clout to tackle climate change. In February 2018 it announced that it would refuse to sign trade deals with countries that did not ratify the Paris climate change agreement.

EU legislation has radically improved our domestic environment. The River Thames, rated as biologically dead fifty years ago, is now home to 125 fish species, as well as seals and porpoises – in no small part because of the EU Water Framework Directive. In the days before EU legislation on waste management, nearly all the UK's waste was disposed of in landfill sites. Today we recycle over 40 per cent of household waste and roughly 50 per cent of commercial and industrial waste. Similar improvements can be found in everything from air quality to conserving the natural habitat.

Brexiters claim that Britain can choose post-Brexit whether to shadow EU law, do less or more, as it thinks fit. But the environment is the quintessential area where across-the-board international collaboration is vital. Birds, fish, water and wind do not respect national frontiers, while national governments are unable to provide the long-term signals or the sheer size of the market that young companies incorporating low-carbon technologies require in order to overcome the reigning dirty technologies. The EU has become the global environmental standard- and regulation-setter.

In summary, the EU is a force for good. It has made Britain stronger, not weaker. In foreign and security policy it has brought us a degree of clout that we would otherwise have lacked – ever more important as China, the US and Russia grow assertively nationalistic and ever more determined to challenge Western democratic, pluralist values. At times like these the West needs to stand together rather than split. The EU has shaped good working conditions and a greener Britain. It has opened up vast opportunities for trade. It has allowed us to work and travel freely across our continent. It has mitigated the growth of inequality between London and the rest of the UK. It has helped parry the worst effects of deindustrialisation.

How could it be that this remarkable expression of European civilisation has been so derided and parodied? Enter Margaret Thatcher, the Brexit right of the Conservative Party, the right-wing media and Mr Nigel Farage.

2

How Mr Farage became leader of the Conservative Party

'We have not successfully rolled back the frontiers of the state in Britain only to see them reimposed at a European level with a European susperstate exercising a new dominance from Brussels.' This proclamation marks the birth of Brexit thirty years ago. It was Margaret Thatcher's declaration of war on the European Union in her Bruges speech of 20 September 1988.

Bruges set off a chain reaction that led to Nigel Farage's reverse takeover of the Conservative Party – the small overwhelming the large, without the cumbersome business of becoming a Conservative MP – and ultimately to the Brexit vote of 23 June 2016. By then, Faragism was the driving philosophy of the Conservative right, and because of the weakness of the rest of the party, the dynamic component of conservatism at large.

On 24 June 2016 David Cameron resigned. Mr Farage became de facto leader of the Conservative Party. Theresa May, who became prime minister, has ever since had to arbitrate between her new leader and the national interest, striking bellicose Brexit negotiating positions to placate Farage and his faction, then partially retreating as she tries to square the party and the public interest. Which is why no one has the faintest idea what 'Brexit means Brexit' really means.

'UP YOURS, DELORS'

There were English nationalists decades and centuries before Bruges.

Vocal right- and left-wing 'anti-Common Market' movements campaigned against Macmillan's and Wilson's applications to join the European Economic Community in the 1960s, and against the Heath government's successful third bid for membership in 1971. Ironically, the observer with the shrewdest appreciation of British Euroscepticism was General Charles de Gaulle, who spent wartime exile in London in a tense relationship with Churchill. As president of France, de Gaulle vetoed the two 1960s applications. 'England in effect is insular,' he declared when snubbing Macmillan in 1963. 'She has, in all her doings, very marked and very original habits and traditions.' It was a partial truth seen through a particular Gaullist lens: France's relationships with Europe are no less complex than England's.

Tony Benn, pitching to the populist left, forced Harold Wilson to hold a referendum three years after Edward Heath signed the Treaty of Rome in 1972. But 'Yes to Europe' won the referendum by two to one, and when Benn, as part of his attempted takeover of the Labour Party, succeeded in committing Labour to 'leaving Europe' in its 1983 manifesto, he lost by a landslide.

It was 'common sense' for Britain to stay in Europe, Thatcher declared, launching the 1975 Conservative 'Yes to Europe' campaign wearing her famous 'Yes to Europe' jumper. Thatcher Mk. I was positively Churchillian:

> It seems to me to display an amazing lack of self-confidence in Britain on the part of some people, that they think that, when no other nation in the Community has lost its national character, Britain in some way will. For hundreds of years the peoples of Britain have been writing history. Do we want future generations to continue to write history or are they simply going to have to read it? If we fail, they will read how extremism won over common sense.

Even in these early 'Common Market' days, Thatcher felt ill at ease with 'European unity'. The daughter of a Grantham grocer, insular and Anglophone, Thatcher's first trip to the continent wasn't until her honeymoon aged twenty-five, and she never visited Germany until becoming leader of the Opposition in 1975. But for now the pull of the Tory grandees, who had fought in the war and knew mainland Europe only too well, was irresistible, and right-wing nationalism was tainted by association with Enoch Powell and his racist, violent, 'rivers of blood' speech of 1968. So although Thatcher famously banged the table to 'get my money back' from Brussels after becoming prime minister in 1979, at first she kept her distance from the nationalist right.

Until the late 1980s there was a European project in which
Thatcher believed. Obliged by the Cold War and American
expectations, she formed a triumvirate with Helmut Kohl and
François Mitterrand to resist the Soviet Union and then to
aid its disintegration under Mikhail Gorbachev. At this stage
she went with the 'economic right' rather than the 'nationalist
right'. Hence the single market – ironically, the one transformational British project in the UK's forty-five years of EU
membership. The aim was to build on Europe's customs
union, eliminating tariff barriers to trade by removing all
'invisible' non-tariff barriers to trade, so creating the world's
largest, richest, single market. It was a breathtaking ambition.

So why the Bruges speech and Thatcher Mk. II? Particularly
when, a few months earlier in 1988, she had spoken of the
wondrous 'single market without barriers – visible or invisible –
giving you direct and unhindered access to the purchasing
power of over 300 million of the world's wealthiest and most
prosperous people. It's not a dream. It's not a vision. It's not
some bureaucrat's plan. It's for real.'

What precipitated Bruges was Jacques Delors, former
French socialist finance minister under Mitterrand, who in
1985 became the strongest and most radical president of the
European Commission since its foundation. Delors pioneered
'social Europe', including new employment rights, which
Thatcher detested. He did so in part – further irony – because
of Thatcher's success in taking on French vested interests in
the whirlwind construction of the single market.

Thatcher was okay with – even briefly enthusiastic about –
the EU while she thought it was mainly about 'markets'. But

not when it moved on to 'social Europe' and 'political integration'. She snapped when Delors came to Bournemouth in early September 1988 to address the Trades Union Congress on the 'social dimension of Europe'. Delors wowed the unions and the left, but Thatcher was appalled. As a direct riposte she promptly rewrote the speech she was due to give to the College of Europe in Bruges twelve days later, inserting the 'superstate' passage. Thatcher would never herself have dreamed of addressing a TUC conference, even in Dorset. She would never have been invited, which gave it added poignancy.

Two years after Bruges, in 1990, Thatcher was forced from power by a revolt of her MPs. She fell partly because of her poll tax and partly owing to her bristling opposition to 'Brussels' and Germany. These were two facets of the same domineering 'control or abolish' philosophy (her hostility to local government at home and to Brussels abroad), as described in chapter 6. Douglas Hurd, her last Foreign Secretary, noted: 'Cabinet now consists of three items: parliamentary affairs, home affairs, and xenophobia.' She was barely restrained even in public. 'We beat the Germans twice and now they are back,' she told fellow heads of government after the fall of the Berlin Wall. It took a war of attrition by Hurd and the Tory grandees to get her to desist from trying to prevent the reunification of Germany.

Unmuzzled out of office, Thatcher railed against her embattled, moderate successor, John Major, for signing the Maastricht Treaty, even though Major secured an opt-out from its key tenet, the single European currency. Symbolically, her last vote in the House of Commons, in 1992, was at the head of a rebellion against Major calling for a referendum on Maastricht. Only twenty Tory MPs supported her, but she had raised her standard and 'Euroscepticism', as it was then called, spread like a plague across her party, especially at the grass roots.

The conversion to Brexit of the Conservative Party was bitterly fought but relentless. The collapse of the Soviet Union in 1991, followed by Maastricht a year later, were key moments. Now that the Soviet threat had evaporated, German predominance and the euro became the issues. While Mitterrand and Kohl sought to situate Germany within a strong, quasi-federal Europe, Thatcher was implacable – 'No, no, no.' Enoch Powell had by now long retired, his last thirteen years in the Commons spent sitting for an Ulster constituency as a Unionist, so it was viable for her to follow her instincts and head a nationalist neoliberal right.

The credo of Thatcherites, young and old, was now simple: 'UP YOURS, DELORS', in the words of the *Sun* headline on 1 November 1990, days before Thatcher's defenestration. 'Sun readers are urged to tell the French fool where to stuff his ECU,' began a rant about plans for a single currency. 'The Sun today calls on its patriotic family to tell the feelthy French to FROG OFF!'

Once Delors and the EU joined her gallery of left-wing enemies, it became a straight case of control or abolish. With Arthur Scargill, Ken Livingstone, the unions and other domestic opposition to Thatcherism now slain, the European Union loomed as the next evil enemy. And this despite the fact that Delors and his successors progressed the single market project quietly and effectively. British companies and the City of London were hugely boosted by the single market – but that cut little ice with the ever more fervent Eurosceptics depicting 'Brussels' as an anti-British plot. By now, Thatcher and the Thatcherites thought that Conservative majorities in the House of Commons were the natural order of things. The first-past-the-post voting system, Tory patriotism, English fear of socialism and the sure support of a powerful right-wing press made them confident that they would more consistently win parliamentary majorities in Britain's winner-take-all political system than Labour; and that Labour, to win, had to move to their agenda anyway. And they weren't far wrong: since 1979 the Tories have won seven elections under four leaders, as against three for Labour under Blair alone – and Blair, declared Margaret Thatcher, was her greatest achievement.

So it was another case of control or abolish. At worst the EU should not grow further; at best it should be broken altogether. However, there was a key proviso: the Thatcherites had also to take complete control over the Conservative Party itself. In the 1990s that was still work in progress.

Windmills

The passage of the Maastricht Treaty into law, after John Major's unexpected 1992 election victory, degenerated into hand-to-hand combat between Major and 'Maastricht rebels' led by Bill Cash and Iain Duncan Smith, egged on by the Iron

Lady herself, who took to phoning Tory MPs to urge them to vote against Major. In July 1993, twenty-six rebels sided with Labour to defeat Major on a procedural motion. When Major reversed this on a motion of confidence, a bitter schism opened among Conservative MPs, which grew and grew until Brexit became the official policy of the Conservative Party on 24 June 2016.

'Brussels' was by now shorthand and scapegoat for everything the Thatcherite right detested. They were generally circumspect in public, making arguments about sovereignty and later immigration, not Thatcherism. Nigel Lawson's revealing boast in the *Financial Times* that 'Brexit gives us a chance to finish the Thatcher revolution' came only in the hubristic aftermath of the 2016 referendum. But Thatcher's visceral anti-state, deregulating, low-tax creed drove Brexit from the outset.

The Tory media, led by Rupert Murdoch's *Sun* and Paul Dacre's *Daily Mail*, went Eurosceptic solidly and early. Margaret Thatcher and the media tycoon Rupert Murdoch were an 'item' for the thirty-five years from her election as Tory leader in 1975 until her death in 2010. There were temperamental bonds: both were impatient Oxford meritocrats from outside the English upper class – from outside England altogether in the case of the Australian newspaper proprietor's son – who reached the top with a ruthless determination to put 'their sort' in charge. But, for Murdoch, it was as much business as culture and politics. Thatcher let Murdoch add the *Times* and *Sunday Times* to his ownership of the *Sun*, helped him break the print unions, and promoted Sky as a rival to the BBC. Leaving No. 10 with him on one occasion, she announced: 'Here is Mr Murdoch, who gives us Sky News, the only unbiased news in the UK.' Anthony Hilton, City Editor of the *Times* in the 1980s, recalled Murdoch saying: 'When I go into Downing Street, they do as I say; when I go to Brussels, they take no notice.'

Paul Dacre took over editorship of the *Daily Mail* from the pro-European Sir David English in 1992, in the midst of Maastricht. Soon the most powerful newspaper editor in Britain, his physical presence, according to one profile, was 'terrifying ... he would rampage through the newsroom with his arms flailing like a windmill, scratching himself manically as he fired himself up.' Even today the ferocity of his swearing inspires fear. And what fired him up more than anything was destroying the 'socialistic' European Union. As with Murdoch, it was a combination of business – 'sensation sells papers' – and conviction. Six years in the United States turned a Leeds University leftie into a born-again Thatcherite: 'America taught me the power of the free market, as opposed to the State, to improve the lives of the vast majority of ordinary people,' he recalls. It's a message Dacre has preached daily, and to five prime ministers over twenty-six years, often in 48-point headlines. And not only to the converted: far more teachers read the *Daily Mail* than the *Guardian*.

In 2002 Thatcher published a 'last will and testament' – her book *Statecraft* – before, increasingly frail, she largely withdrew from public life. It was Bruges on steroids:

That such an unnecessary and irrational project as building a European superstate was ever embarked upon will
seem in future years to be perhaps the greatest folly of
the modern era. And that Britain, with her traditional
strengths and global destiny, should ever have been part of
it will appear a political error of historic magnitude.

In 1995, the Eurosceptics challenged John Major for the
party leadership. His opponent John Redwood's programme
was pure Thatcher: hanging, keeping the Royal Yacht, big tax
cuts all round. Redwood got eighty-nine votes, a new Brexit
high, rallying not only activists but also, crucially, Thatcherite
party donors. Property developer Paul Sykes withdrew funding
from the central party and began solely funding Eurosceptic
candidates; he would go on to be a key funder of the United
Kingdom Independence Party – UKIP.

In April 1996, Iain Duncan Smith secured sixty-six
Conservative MPs to support a private member's bill giving
Parliament the power to overrule the European Court of
Justice. Two months later seventy-six Tories supported Bill
Cash's bill requiring a referendum on the UK's membership of
the EU if further powers were ceded to Brussels. Eurosceptic
groups and think tanks were now sprouting everywhere,
including the European Reform Group, the Fresh Starters, and
the Bruges Group. Euroscepticism was moving into the Tory
mainstream; there were few countervailing arguments on the
right, and the generation of Tory MPs who had served in the
war was steadily dying out.

By 1997, the electorate had sickened of the Tories, their

divisions and the evident fissures in British society that Thatcherism had inflicted. The youthful Tony Blair offered a fresh non-socialist alternative, proclaiming 'one nation', and the Tories were reduced to a rump. However, among the survivors, Thatcherites and Thatcherism reigned supreme. Major's successor, William Hague, was one of them. In a speech drafted by Daniel Hannan in the 2001 election, Hague took official Tory Euroscepticism to a new high. Labour would turn Britain into 'foreign land' for the British; this was the last chance for the British people to 'remain sovereign in their own country'.

After Tony Blair's second landslide in 2001, Hague was succeeded by Iain Duncan Smith, a darling of the Eurosceptics. IDS's leadership soon imploded from sheer incompetence; he was replaced by Michael Howard, similarly Thatcherite, just more capable. In these successive leadership contests the most qualified and electorally popular figure was the unThatcherite Ken Clarke: jazz-loving man about town, MP for the East Midlands city of Nottingham, and successful chancellor under Major. But every time, Clarke's Europeanism made him unelectable by rank-and-file Tory members, who since 1998 selected the party leader.

In 2005, David Cameron became the fifth Tory leader to face Tony Blair. A former PR executive, he knew that the Tories' obsessive image had to go, and told his first party conference to 'stop banging on about Europe'. But he too told the party he was Thatcherite – by now there was no other credible Toryism on offer. As a pledge of allegiance he withdrew Tory MEPs from the main centre-right European People's Party group in the European Parliament; instead they allied with far-right populists including Latvian fascists and Austrians in favour of banning gay pride marches. Leaving the EPP typified Cameron's policy for his eleven years as Tory leader: periodically throwing red meat to the Eurosceptics, while hoping to contain the consequences. He couldn't.

Midwives

The two most successful politicians since Margaret Thatcher are an unlikely pair: Tony Blair and Nigel Farage. In complementary ways they were the midwives of Brexit.

Tony Blair spoke French, learned in a Paris bar. He spent most of his holidays in France and Italy and saw himself as a modern European. In his early years in No. 10 he lived up to this in two key respects: his robust action against Serbian dictator Slobodan Milošević's genocide in Kosovo, and his championing of a modernising 'third way' brand of social democracy which influenced all of Europe's left parties to some degree.

However, by the end of his decade in No. 10, Blair had opened several doors to Brexit. The first was his decision to stay out of the European Single Currency. Although Blair periodically toyed with attempting to join the euro, with bouts of feverish strategising, he never came close to actually doing so.

The first years of the Blair leadership were spent partly hoping, partly predicting that the euro wouldn't happen; a repeat of the misjudgement of Anthony Eden in the 1950s that the Treaty of Rome wouldn't amount to anything even if it was signed. Had Britain joined the euro at the outset, Blair could have helped shape the rules and membership; he might even have secured the European Central Bank for London, a badge of economic rectitude that he and Gordon Brown sought instead by giving the Bank of England control of setting interest rates, a modest reform dressed up as a bold one. Membership was only seriously contemplated once euro notes and coins were issued in 2002, by which time the best – maybe only – political opportunity to join had passed. At the time, the economic arguments for joining were evenly balanced, with Britain's flexible labour markets reckoned to allow potential economic shocks to be absorbed, so permitting all the advantages of a competitive and stable exchange rate to be enjoyed. The offsetting concern was the inability to use interest rates to check potential overheating in Britain's housing market – in the event a freedom never exercised. But there was no political will to join, and the balanced Treasury assessment of 2003 was presented as negatively as possible.

The real reason that Blair kept out of the euro is summed up by the very first page of the visitors' book at Chequers, the prime minister's country residence, after he took office. The page is headed: 'Saturday 3rd May 1997: Lunch'. Beneath are four signatures: Tony Blair, Cherie Booth QC, Rupert Murdoch and Alastair Campbell. Blair was simply not prepared to take on the right-wing media over the euro or Europe, and the case was never made.

Blair also, unwittingly, advanced the cause of a Brexit referendum. While Thatcher and Major did not hold a single referendum between them, Blair routinely deployed referendums as an arm's-length device to manage controversial issues. Scottish and Welsh devolution, a mayor of London, even a toothless assembly for the North-East of England: all were made subject to referendums despite his 1997 and 2001 landslides. Europe fell into this pattern. In order to appease Murdoch, soon after becoming Labour leader in 1994 Blair announced that any proposal for euro membership would be subject to a referendum. By 1997 this was paraded as part of a 'triple lock' – the other two locks were cabinet and Parliament – against any 'premature' or 'unwise' decision to join the euro, as if a Blair government might need protecting from itself.

Cameron, who lifted so much from the Blair playbook, was to use referendums in a similar way. It paid off on electoral reform, where he destroyed Nick Clegg's dreams in a referendum in 2011. Three years later he won a referendum gamble on Scottish independence by a smaller margin. Brexit was third time unlucky.

To resolve another right-wing media storm, Blair proposed a referendum on the European constitution recommended in 2004 by the European Convention chaired by former French president Giscard d'Estaing. Jacques Chirac saved him, losing a referendum on the same issue in France before the British referendum was held. Blair refused to hold a referendum on the replacement Treaty of Lisbon, which would probably have been lost. A referendum on Lisbon became a key Cameron commitment. It was averted because Lisbon had just been ratified by the time he took office in 2010, but a Brexit referendum moved a step closer. Brexit Tories and the right-wing media now had a betrayal narrative.

Blair's invasion of Iraq alongside George W. Bush in 2003, in the teeth of opposition from France and Germany, was a further boost to Brexit. The idea of Britain as a twenty-first-century bridge between the United States and Europe collapsed on the killing fields of Baghdad and Basra. 'European foreign policy', a key part of the Lisbon Treaty, was an impossibility while Blair virtually ceased speaking to Jacques Chirac and Gerhard Schroeder, accompanied by intense anti-French and anti-German rhetoric echoing the attack on 'old Europe' by Donald Rumsfeld, Bush's unpopular Defense Secretary. It was the strategic misjudgement of his premiership. Blair wanted his Falklands; he got his Suez.

Blair's last contribution to Brexit was decisive: allowing unrestricted immigration from central and eastern Europe after 2004.

When Poland and seven other central and East European countries joined the EU in 2004, a seven-year transitional period applied during which other member states could restrict their citizens' right to work. Blair decided not to apply these transitional controls. The UK was one of only three states, and by far the largest, not to do so. Overnight, Britain became the strongest magnet for voluntary migration in post-war Europe as central and eastern Europeans – largely poor but educated and motivated – flocked over.

Blair had been badly caught out. Home Office predictions were that around thirteen thousand Poles and others would come to the UK every year. This was based on the assumption that all fifteen pre-existing members of the EU would open up their labour markets immediately, and that East Europeans would more likely emigrate to countries nearer home. At this level of immigration, the UK's competitiveness would be boosted, and Britain's reputation for being open and pro-European would be promoted, with no apparent downside.

It was a fateful political call. Immigration from Poland was unexpectedly large. 'Net migration' – the difference between Brits leaving the UK and continental EU citizens coming to the UK – escalated to 110,000 a year by 2010, and in the three years up to the 2016 referendum climbed to 160,000. The public didn't distinguish between EU and non-EU immigration; it was all the same in Spalding and Sunderland. Nigel Farage was more than happy to blame it all on the EU. So too the refugee crisis precipitated by the Arab Spring of 2010, then dramatically worsened by the Syrian civil war after 2012. Britain accepted very few Syrian refugees, but that's not what the public thought, particularly if they listened to Farage and read the *Daily Mail*. By the time of the referendum, all immigrants and refugees were conflated into one huge, dishevelled army on the march towards Dover across open borders at the behest of the European Union.

The visceral opposition to post-2004 immigration can only be understood alongside the social memory of mass immigration from the Commonwealth in the 1950s and 1960s. It was black Commonwealth immigration that created Enoch Powell as a populist racist. 'As I look ahead, I am filled with foreboding; like the Roman, I seem to see the River Tiber foaming with much blood ... In this country in fifteen or twenty years' time the black man will have the whip hand over the white man' – Powell's infamous April 1968 speech in Birmingham, sixteen days after the assassination of Martin Luther King, was the most notorious by a leading politician since Chamberlain returned from Munich and announced 'peace in our time'. Powell was sacked by Heath from the Tory shadow cabinet, and historians look back on his successful ostracism, despite huge popular support, as a catastrophe averted. But the rejection was of Powell's rhetoric, not his policy.

Just five weeks before 'rivers of blood', large-scale immigration into Britain was halted overnight by emergency legislation rushed through Parliament in three days, supported by both major parties. 'We are about to discuss one of the greatest issues of our time, an issue which can tear us apart or unite us,' were Labour home secretary James Callaghan's dramatic words on introducing the legislation in the Commons. He went on: 'It would be irresponsible not to legislate on this vast issue of whether this country could afford in any circumstances to envisage the prospect of an invasion.'

Callaghan's 1968 Commonwealth Immigrants Act took immigration out of British politics so successfully that thirty-six years later a new generation of politicians with no political memory of the 1960s failed to appreciate how quickly immigration can turn toxic if the pace of change is too fast. They soon learned.

'A wind-up merchant, bloody-minded and difficult'

Like Enoch Powell, Nigel Farage was a populist demagogue years in the making.

The origins of his party, UKIP, lie in the fringe organisations that sprouted after Thatcher's Bruges speech. Shortly before the 1992 election Alan Sked, a London School of Economics professor, left the Bruges Group, which he considered too loyal to John Major's fainthearts, to found the Anti-Federalist League. In the 1992 election Sked won just 117 votes in Bath, the seat lost by Chris Patten, who went on to become vice-president of the European Commission. A year later the Anti-Federalist League founded UKIP. The founding meeting largely comprised anti-European academics, with two notable additions: Julian Lewis of Conservative Central Office, later a Tory MP, and one Nigel Farage.

Farage grew up in awe of Margaret Thatcher. He joined the Tories in 1978 after Keith Joseph, Thatcher's radical free market mentor, spoke at his south London public school, Dulwich. A brash public school semi-rebel – a self-confessed 'wind-up merchant', 'bloody-minded' and 'difficult' – Farage planned to coin it in the City without bothering with university. As he headed to a City metal trading floor in 1982, Thatcherism became his philosophy of life.

By now a nuance-free Thatcherite contemptuous of the EU, Farage got active in the Bruges Group in the late 1980s, and through it UKIP. 'You've hit on the right word – nation,' he declared in his first election campaign in 1994. 'We are the only party trying to stop all you fight for being thrown out

of the window. We are witnessing a case of national suicide.'
He took Thatcher's line on John Major: weak and useless.
Euroscepticism was the reclamation of Thatcherism.

'The more I read about the history of the Tory Party or politics, you realise that Thatcher actually wasn't Conservative at
all, she was a radical economic liberal,' Farage said in one interview. Asked if that was what he was, he replied: 'Absolutely.'
He would later say, 'I was never a Tory. I am a Thatcherite ...
If you look at TV footage of Mrs Thatcher being interviewed
in the eighties it actually takes your breath away,' he said. 'She
had conviction, passion, belief. She was forthright. She spoke
in a language that ordinary people could understand.'

In 1994, aged thirty, the same age as Tony Blair when first
elected to Parliament in 1983, Farage stood for UKIP in the
Eastleigh by-election in Hampshire. He polled just 952 votes,
on the same day as European elections in which UKIP won
just 1 per cent. UKIP vied for fringe attention with the billion-
aire financier Sir James Goldsmith and his Referendum Party,
set up in the same year, whose sole objective was an in/out EU
referendum. Goldsmith had everything UKIP lacked: money,
connections, and name recognition for its leader.

Farage soon developed an instinct for campaigning and the
limelight.

In the 1997 election he notched up 3332 votes in Salisbury.
He was rising to the top of the UKIP pack, but that didn't
mean much. Then he had two strokes of luck. Two months
after Tony Blair's landslide, Goldsmith died. His Referendum
Party disintegrated and Farage became the principal legatee.
His second, equally vital, break was Blair's decision to change

the electoral system for the 1999 Euro elections from first-past-the-post to proportional representation.

Blair's switch to PR for Euro elections was mainly designed to appease the Lib Dems and the 'pluralists' within the Labour Party. But as with Mitterrand's ill-fated tactical decision to switch the French electoral system to PR in the mid-1980s, intended to wrong-foot his right-wing rival Jacques Chirac, but which rocket-boosted Jean-Marie Le Pen's National Front, the main beneficiary was the populist right. UKIP now secured seats, status and salaries in Brussels in a way they couldn't at Westminster, partly because of first-past-the-post but also because in 'real' Westminster elections their vote was invariably too low and evenly spread to win seats. Euro elections, by contrast, were protest votes, and what better protest vehicle than a populist party whose mantra was vilification of the European institutions whose perceived extravagance symbolised the elite that people wanted to protest against in the first place?

By now well funded by former Tory donors, UKIP fielded candidates in all eleven constituencies for the 1999 Euro elections. It was first mid-term blues for New Labour. The Tories came first; UKIP was fourth with 6.5 per cent, but under the regional list PR system, that was enough to elect three UKIP MEPs, one of them Nigel Farage. And so began his nineteen years' membership of 'a parliament I want no part of, under a system I despise ... blinking into the cameras at one in the morning saying how proud I was', he recalled. When in 2019 he completes two decades as – possibly – one of the UK's last MEPs, he will draw a lifetime Euro pension of £73,000.

Equipped with a platform, profile, quick wits, and adoring Brexit sugar daddies like Paul Sykes and later Arron Banks, Farage took control of UKIP. In 2006 he stopped trading metals and became UKIP leader. There were rocky patches. The charismatic ex-Labour MP turned chat-show host Robert Kilroy-Silk had a brief flirtation with the party when his TV career abruptly halted in 2004. 'Kilroy' became a UKIP MEP but lost to Farage in a clash of egos, as did UKIP's defector from the Tory benches in the Commons, Douglas Carswell, a decade later.

Honing his 'chap-about-town-with-a-pint-and-a-fag' image, Farage needed a breakthrough issue. 'Brussels' itself wasn't helpful on this score, because under the shrewd leadership of the former Portuguese centre-right prime minister Manuel Barroso, the Commission in the 2000s got on patiently with 'enlargement' of the EU to the east and deepening the single market, including the path-breaking 2006 Services Directive and a focus on competitiveness. Both were British projects, hard to carp about from the free-market right. There were concessions to British concerns to promote inter-governmentalism and retreat from supranationalism. Lisbon also introduced the Early Warning System which allowed national parliaments to object to proposed EU legislation where they felt it violated the principle of 'subsidiarity'. None of this offered Farage the red meat he needed.

There was one open goal: immigration. In his early UKIP years, Farage trod warily on immigration, mindful of Enoch Powell. 'He clearly lost the centre ground with the violence of his language. I have been very conscious not to make the same mistake,' he said candidly. Instead, grasping the politics of Thatcher, including her nuanced admiration of Enoch Powell, he operated by nods and winks – until his chance came to jump on to Blair's failure to impose transitional controls on the East Europeans in 2004. Then, adopting almost identical language of 'swamping' that Thatcher had used in the run-up to the 1979 election, he attacked the Conservatives, as much as the Labour government, for letting Britain be 'swamped'. 'The Europhiles claim that an enlarged EU will bring economic benefits to the UK,' he said. 'I rather doubt this, though it will bring a flood of people from Eastern Europe seeking benefits.' Britain was 'FULL UP', UKIP's June 2004 Euro election manifesto declared, two months after the flow of immigrants had started. It needed 'freedom from overcrowding' and a target of zero net migration. On the back of a £2 million campaign devised by ex-Clinton strategist Dick Morris, UKIP quadrupled its number of MEPs to twelve, taking 16 per cent of the vote and beating the Liberal Democrats into fourth place. In September 2004 UKIP took 10 per cent of the vote and pushed the Tories into fourth place in the Hartlepool by-election, on Peter Mandelson's appointment to the European Commission.

Farage soon had the Tories in tow. Tacking hard right, Michael Howard ran the Conservative 2005 election campaign on the slogan 'Are you thinking what we're thinking?', beneath pictures of immigrants. It was a short step to Farage's 'Breaking Point' poster of the 2016 referendum featuring a queue of dark-faced 'Syrian refugees' heading remorselessly out of the poster towards the viewer.

'Fruit cakes, loonies and closet racists' – or not

As Tory leader after 2005, David Cameron dropped Howard's racist innuendo. But so too, for the most part, did Farage, by now a highly skilled populist. Farage kept 'clear purple water' between UKIP and the out-and-out racist British National Party, which outperformed UKIP in parts of urban England in local elections in the mid-2000s, and its thuggish leader Nick Griffin. A strong line on 'radical Islam' was one way through. Farage zeroed in on Sharia law and proposed to ban the burka. He contrived to embroil himself in a row about inviting the populist anti-Islamic Dutch politician Geert Wilders to Parliament.

In the 2005 general election, Blair's last, UKIP polled 2.2 per cent – not a breakthrough, but twice the Green vote. In the first English by-election of the 2005 Parliament, eight months after Cameron became Tory leader, Farage took third place from Labour in Bromley and Chislehurst in affluent south London. It's often remarked that Farage never won a seat at a by-election or a general election, as if this was a handicap. But it had the paradoxical advantage of making him constantly available to fight them, which he did – seven times in all – from his already secure platform in Brussels.

From that moment on, Cameron lived in perpetual fear of a UKIP surge. For much of his five years as leader of the Opposition (2005–10) it was far from clear that he would survive, still less win a general election. His strategy was 'Brexit-lite': as well as leaving the centre-right EPP group in the European Parliament, he promised a referendum on

Lisbon, pledged to reform or repatriate everything from the social chapter to 'free movement' of people, the Common Agricultural Policy and the Common Fisheries Policy. He also speculated that he might somehow – though he knew not how – 'restore' the sovereignty of Parliament over the European Court of Justice. Everything short of the final concession: a Brexit referendum. Jibes about UKIP – 'a bunch of fruitcakes, loonies and closet racists' – were soon dropped.

The 2009 parliamentary expenses scandal, which erupted shortly before the Euro elections of that year, came as a gift to UKIP. Norman Tebbit, ardent Brexiter and Tory chairman under Margaret Thatcher, explicitly urged Tories to vote UKIP. Gordon Brown's Labour Party was pushed into third place and UKIP won thirteen seats, increasing its vote to 16.5 per cent.

Hence Cameron's pledge in his 2010 manifesto to cut net immigration to just 'tens of thousands'. Net immigration from all sources was at 250,000 by 2010. With Farage committed to zero, Cameron's stance was statistically about two-thirds of the way towards UKIP, which summed up his Brexit-lite positioning. Labour was under pressure too, harshly exhibited by Gordon Brown's disastrous encounter with Gillian Duffy in Rochdale during the 2010 election, when he was caught on microphone calling her a 'bigoted woman'. Mrs Duffy responded: 'You can't say anything about the immigrants and these eastern Europeans what are coming in.'

It was a winding but not particularly slow road from Cameron's entry into Downing Street in May 2010 to the referendum of 23 June 2016. The lack of a Tory majority put a Brexit referendum on the back burner, but it never left the stove. Brexit-lite endured, crucially in the form of a bill to require referendums on all future EU treaty changes, agreed with his coalition partner Nick Clegg and the Liberal Democrats who, fearing a UKIP surge in their West Country heartlands, themselves wanted to sound tough on 'Brussels'. This did not satisfy the right, of course. In October 2011, eighty-one Tory MPs voted for a Brexit referendum, a rebellion twice as large as any against John Major on Maastricht. 'From that day onwards it was inevitable that we were going to have a referendum,' declared Peter Bone, a self-appointed leader of the awkward squad.

Tellingly, even Nick Clegg's Liberal Democrats were by now committed in principle to a Brexit referendum at an undefined future date. By 2012 UKIP was polling 7–8 per cent. Michael Fabricant, a vice-chairman of the Conservative Party, spoke for most Tory activists in calling for an electoral pact with UKIP around a Brexit referendum. Fabricant pointed out that in twenty-one seats in the 2010 election the UKIP vote was greater than the Conservative margin of loss: UKIP was 'a major contributory factor to the Conservatives failing to win an overall majority'.

The continuing effects of the financial crisis in 2008/9, which spilled into a crisis of the Eurozone in general and Greek debt in particular, and later overlapped with the Syrian refugee crisis, became a backdrop of alleged EU failure. The EU was caricatured as sclerotic, an economic corpse and, over Greece, heartless; Germany was the sinister spider at the centre of a web of austerity policies prolonging the European

recession and imposing impossible economic terms on helpless
Greece. This was proof positive, repeated by the far left and
Eurosceptic right alike, of the degree to which a centralised
European Union, preoccupied with over-ambitious pan-
European policies like the euro, was an elite project aiming to
subvert the peoples of Europe.

There was an alternative narrative that rarely surfaced.
The scale of the British financial crisis was no less awesome,
and the recovery from the 2008/9 recession the weakest for a
century. The scale of the deficit reduction launched voluntarily in Britain by Cameron and Osborne was as fierce outside
the Eurozone as that demanded of Greece, Portugal and
Ireland within it. Yet owing to the euro, the domino effect of
collapsing banking systems that had prompted the slump of
the 1930s was not repeated: the European Central Bank saved
the European banking system. Although Greece undertook a
fierce programme of economic retrenchment, the bulk of its
debt was forgiven, and for all the crises, its populist parties
gained little traction in wanting to leave either the euro or the
EU. Greece was substantially the author of its own misfor-
tunes, and EU membership buttressed it against Turkey. In
2018, the beneficiaries of a strong economic recovery, the EU
and euro have passed the sternest of tests. And the refugee
crisis that engulfed southern Europe and Germany did not
stem from any EU action: it was the knock-on effect of the
invasion of Iraq a decade earlier.

Cameron, succumbing to the prejudices of his party, chose
only to indulge the critics and never made the counter case,
instead latching on to openings made available by the ongoing

crisis of the Eurozone to try to force concessions from EU leaders. Within months of taking office he sought to make British support for treaty changes to shore up the monetary union (which did not affect Britain at all outside the euro) conditional upon the UK being allowed to opt out of majority voting for financial sector rules within the single market. He wanted to sell this to his Eurosceptic wing as a victory over Europe. However, the only effect was to infuriate Chancellor Merkel, who saw this as student union politics in the face of a major European crisis. She refused point-blank. Britain was isolated at the European Council at the end of 2011 in what Sir Ivan Rogers, Britain's ambassador to the EU, describes as a 'moment of near-terminal rupture'. Merkel and French president Nicolas Sarkozy circumvented Britain by doing a deal among the seventeen Eurozone members by means of an intergovernmental treaty. This was agreed among them at an EPP leaders' meeting in Marseille, from which Cameron was tellingly absent because he had left the EPP.

In coalition with the Liberal Democrats after 2010, and thereby safeguarded against having to act on the worst of its own prejudices, the Conservative Party grew ever more crazed about Europe. Brexit-lite Cameron sought any emollient bone to throw not only to his Eurosceptic MPs but to the ragingly sceptic Conservative constituency party associations, their elderly heads turned by the torrent of anti-EU propaganda from the right-wing press. In 2012 a 'balance of competences' review was launched by Cameron with the explicit aim of establishing that the legal powers and responsibilities of the EU were excessive, thus necessitating a renegotiation of EU treaties. It remains the most comprehensive audit of the workings of the EU ever produced, based on thirty-two volumes and three thousand pages of evidence submitted by 1500 independent sources. But it did not deliver as Cameron hoped. Far from any sweeping condemnation of the EU, the review found that the EU served British interests pretty well, with any compromises on sovereignty more than made up for by policy gains with powerful economic and social benefits. Indeed, British business was very satisfied.

Rather than convey these findings to the public, the government filed them away. As the House of Lords European Affairs Committee, chaired by former Tory minister Lord Boswell, put it acidly: if the purpose of the review was to 'ground the public debate on the EU on a strong evidence base', this seemed 'an unrealistic aim, as long as the public are unaware of the Review's existence ... there is no point spending up to £5 million of public money on an excellent review and then burying it. People need to know the facts about the UK–EU relationship.' Such was the ignorance that even the Remain campaign barely mentioned the government's own assessment in the 2016 referendum debate.

Given the steady build-up of Europhobia under Thatcher and Farage, Cameron's fateful announcement of a Brexit referendum in his Bloomberg speech of 23 January 2013 seemed almost inevitable. It wasn't a one-off error but the logical conclusion of the Brexit-lite policy he had followed since 2005. Revealingly, although George Osborne has subsequently claimed to have been opposed to a Brexit referendum, none of Cameron's lieutenants tried hard to stop him, Osborne included. They too saw further appeasement of Farage as unavoidable. Even in retrospect they hold the same line. In his memoirs Sir Oliver Letwin, Cameron's policy chief and a Tory frontbencher and adviser going right back to Thatcher's policy unit (where he devised the poll tax), says that the Brexit referendum was 'right in principle and inevitable in practice'. 'If we failed to guarantee a referendum, we were more than likely to lose enough seats to UKIP to deprive us of an overall majority, in which case, we would end up depending on UKIP support in Parliament, the condition of which would of course (ironically) be the holding of a referendum.' This logic bows to the premise that Farage was now the arbiter of Tory politics and electoral fortunes.

Farage proclaimed 'a tremendous victory'. His verdict in retrospect: 'It was so obvious to me at the time of Bloomberg that any argument that I should have worked from within the Conservative Party would never have worked – and actually the UKIP tactic of fighting and taking votes from the outside had worked.' Now he moved in for the kill, true to the words of Kipling, beloved by Enoch Powell: 'If once you have paid him the Dane-geld, you never get rid of the Dane.' In the June 2014 Euro elections UKIP got its best-ever result: 26 per cent and twenty-four seats. The Conservatives came third, the first time ever in a national election that they had not come first or second. Three months later, just after the 2014 Tory Party conference, two Tory MPs dramatically defected to UKIP. Both held their seats in by-elections, provoking panic in Downing Street that more Tory MPs might defect at any moment. The pressure was on Labour too: on the same day in October 2014 as the by-election that returned Douglas Carswell as UKIP MP for Clacton in left-behind coastal Essex, Labour held off UKIP by only 617 votes in a by-election in similarly deprived Greater Manchester.

By now, Farage was playing daily variations on his anti-immigrant riff. He told *Newsweek* in November 2014 that immigrants with HIV should not be admitted to Britain. By the 2015 election campaign this was amplified to the false claim that 60 per cent of those diagnosed with HIV in Britain were foreign and exploiting the NHS. The 'Australian points system' was UKIP's magic cure to keep high-skilled migrants while weeding out the 'HIV tourists'.

In the run-up to the 2015 election, immigration consistently ranked in polls as one of the top three issues that faced the country, often coming top. The three mainstream parties did their best not to talk about it – 'Mass immigration . . . has been all but airbrushed from this election, even by the Tories', the *Daily Mail* blazed halfway through the election – but that did not abate public sentiment.

By early 2015 UKIP was polling 17 per cent and predicting it would win up to twenty seats in the coming general election. Its appeal went far wider than just Europe and immigration. As Lord Ashcroft noted in one of his poll summaries, UKIP's primary attraction was that they 'will say things that need to be said but others are scared to say'.

It was an article of faith among Tory pollsters in the run-up to the 2015 election that a UKIP vote of more than 10 per cent would make it impossible for the Conservatives to secure a majority. A panicked Cameron tacked further right. Absurd as it was, he repeated his 'tens of thousands' immigration pledge for the 2015 election. He had long since stopped calling UKIP 'closet racists' and was now referring to them jovially in private as 'my little purple friends'. Cameron made a Brexit referendum a 'red line' in any future coalition negotiations with the Lib Dems. When challenged directly by Farage in the one televised leaders' debate of the campaign: 'Do you accept or not that in your renegotiation free movement is not up for discussion?', he replied: 'I don't accept that.'

In the event UKIP did surge in the May 2015 election, to 12.6 per cent, by far its highest poll in any general election, pushing the Lib Dems into a distant fourth place. Through the quirks of first-past-the-post, Cameron nonetheless won a majority of seats on just 36.9 per cent of the vote.

But with Clegg and the Lib Dems eviscerated, Cameron's Brexit referendum 'red line' now applied only to himself.

Breaking point

One of Cameron's first acts on forming, in May 2015, the first purely Conservative government in eighteen years was to legislate for a Brexit referendum. Labour and the Lib Dems voted for it, in deference to the Tory/UKIP landslide, and it passed the Commons by the overwhelming majority of 544 to fifty-three votes, with only the SNP voting against.

Like Harold Wilson forty years earlier, Cameron set out to secure a 'new deal' with the European Union that could be sold as a favourable renegotiation of terms in a referendum.

His problem was twofold. First, Britain had already secured almost all the opt-outs and concessions possible, along with greatly strengthened measures against further integration; and second, his party and his media had created impossible benchmarks for success that in the event could only be achieved by leaving.

Cameron won some extra powers to limit immigration within the EU, which fell well short of the much-vaunted 'emergency brake', along with a cluster of largely declaratory and technical concessions like removing the objective of 'ever closer union' from Britain's treaty commitments. The net effect was very different from Wilson's in 1975. Although Wilson did not secure fundamental treaty changes – he didn't want any – he got an improved deal on New Zealand lamb and butter which he paraded successfully as cheaper food in the shops and playing fair by our Commonwealth 'kith and kin'. Cameron had no parallel gains to parade.

Cameron should have demanded more, and might have secured the 'emergency brake', had he done a Thatcher and played really tough. But he didn't try. He even foolishly told Merkel he could win the referendum without the 'emergency brake'. Moreover, he was keen to move quickly. Another Syrian and North African refugee surge was looming, and his party was growing daily more Faragist. He thought time was his enemy.

So on 20 February 2016, less than ten months after the general election, a Brexit referendum was called for 23 June.

From day one, Cameron was on the back foot. The argument about a 'reformed' European Union was not so much lost as never even made. Steve Baker, leader of the Brexit brigade on the Tory backbenches, called his renegotiation 'like polishing poo'. To the *Daily Mail* it was 'THE GREAT DELUSION'. 'WHO DO EU THINK YOU ARE KIDDING MR CAMERON,' opined Murdoch's *Sun*, beside a picture of a steaming pile of manure. The *Mail* ran anti-immigration stories on its front page on seventeen of the twenty-three days before the referendum.

Cameron was typically blasé about the referendum arrangements. He allowed an electoral quango, under pressure from the Faragists, to change the question from 'yes/no' to 'leave/ remain'. This decision alone probably lost the referendum, given its narrow outcome. He also lined up with the Faragists in refusing to insert a threshold for a Leave vote to take effect: only 38 per cent of the registered electorate voted Leave. He refused to allow sixteen- and seventeen-year-olds to vote, although they had been given the vote in the Scottish independence referendum two years previously and were strongly pro-EU.

No requirement was demanded of Leave to set out their stall so that voters would know what Leave entailed. The voteLeavetakecontrol website explicitly argued that Britain would stay in the single market via membership of the European Economic Area – yet leaving them became a red line subsequently. And Cameron failed to legislate for any parliamentary or legal process to be followed in the event of a Leave majority, including a subsequent referendum on the Brexit deal itself, essential to allow the 'sovereign people' to consider the actual divorce deal resulting from any 'instruction' to Parliament to negotiate one. It was this critical omission that bequeathed the ongoing parliamentary crisis about defining and delivering Brexit.

It was immigration that decisively soured opinion. On the eve of the referendum, 63 per cent believed that refugees were one of the most important issues then facing the country, compared with just 39 per cent saying the same for the NHS, or 33 per cent the economy.

A British Social Attitudes survey found that 43 per cent wanted Britain to stay in a reformed EU. Much of the EU referendum came down to whether or not Cameron's deal qualified, in the minds of the British people, as 'reform', particularly on immigration. It did not. According to Survation, on the most important issue, immigration, just 26 per cent felt that his renegotiation would reduce immigration, while 60 per cent believed it would make no difference. A clear majority believed his reforms did not go far enough. Whilst in 1975 the government's renegotiation was one of the reasons why support for 'In' doubled in the six months before the referendum, Cameron's renegotiation was an unqualified electoral failure. Forty-seven per cent said it would make no difference to their vote, and 31 per cent said it would make them more likely to vote to leave.

A study of 268 referendums since 1990 finds that in 69 per cent of them, the 'change' option won. Dissatisfaction with the status quo in 'left out' Britain made Britain ripe for such a 'change' vote.

The campaign itself was a textbook disaster. The day after its launch Cameron lost the then most popular Tory in the country, outgoing mayor of London Boris Johnson, to the leadership of the Leave campaign alongside Farage, plus a quarter of his cabinet. Johnson spent the campaign on a bus emblazoned with 'We send the EU £350 million a week – let's fund our NHS instead'. He was cheered by Tory activists wherever he went, Faragists to the core. Quitting the EU had long become an article of faith among the mostly retired Tory membership, yearning for a better Thatcherite yesterday.

Nor was Labour much help, distancing itself from a cross-party platform in the belief this would tar it with a Tory brush. Jeremy Corbyn, the Labour leader, was only semi-convinced in the EU cause and offered none of the passion he was to exhibit in the 2017 general election.

On 16 June, Farage unveiled his 'Breaking Point' poster. A few hours later, the Labour MP Jo Cox was murdered in broad daylight by a far-right nationalist extremist in her West Yorkshire constituency.

Exactly a week later, 33,577,342 electors, the largest number in the history of the United Kingdom, voted.

Shortly after dawn on 24 June, David Cameron announced on the steps of 10 Downing Street that he would respect 'the instruction of the British people' to leave the European Union. He also announced his resignation.

Nigel Farage was having breakfast at the Ritz with Freddie Barclay, owner of the Ritz and the *Telegraph*.

On 13 July Theresa May succeeded David Cameron as prime minister. But it was Mr Farage who had become leader of the Conservative Party.

3

The lion without the roar

Britain has begun an argument over its identity and direction that is not going to disappear, whatever happens on 29 March 2019.

Emotions over Europe are at their most raw in attitudes to the Union Jack and the European flag. Before 2016 the English did not much go in for flags, beyond the far-right fringe. Now flags are everywhere, and they have become very emotive. Flying the EU flag or painting it on your face as young people increasingly do at rallies and concerts is derided as evidence of 'split allegiance' in the words of Boris Johnson.

For Johnson, only one flag should fly in Britain: the Union Jack. But for British Europeans the Union Jack and the European flag are two symbols of the same identity and common citizenship, British and European. There is no tension in flying them both. However, this common identity is deeply contested and goes to the heart of Brexit.

Leave tapped into this ambivalence. Survey evidence finds

that within the EU, the UK ranks last in terms of how many of its nationals identify as European. While two-thirds of British do not identify as European, only 30 per cent of Germans do not. Fewer British nationals live outside the UK in the EU than proportionally do the nationals of any other EU country. More Britons live in Australia than in all twenty-seven other EU countries combined.

Yet many Britons – perhaps most – had come to an accommodation with the EU. They did not especially love it, but saw its value and did not hate it either. Indeed, the overwhelming prominence of the EU and matters European is very recent. Even among Tories who are traditionally more Eurosceptic, Europe was a secondary issue just eight years ago. The 2010 *British Election Study* found a mere 0.7 per cent of Conservative voters identifying Europe as the most important issue facing the country. In polling of the wider population, in 2012 only 6 per cent in an Ipsos MORI survey thought the EU or Europe was the most important issue facing Britain; at the beginning of 2013, at the time of David Cameron's Bloomberg speech, the EU still did not make the top ten issues facing the country. Passionate Euroscepticism was a minority pursuit – about as popular as fox-hunting.

But lack of interest in the EU, together with a virtual absence of citizenship education in schools, allowed wild ignorance of the EU to take hold. It was widely held, for example, that Britain contributed as much as 20 per cent of its national income to the EU budget – the actual figure is closer to 1 per cent.

Emergency services

What swung indifference to the EU into active opposition was immigration, along with the belief that David Cameron's deal would make little difference. It was overwhelmingly the trigger issue. In Weymouth, a coastal town and social-mobility coldspot, the UKIP candidate in 2015 was former merchant navy captain Malcolm Shakesby. While in 1997 he had courted Tory votes by playing the sovereignty card, asking if Brussels should rule Britain, eighteen years later his campaign on the council estates of Weymouth and Portland had one message: immigration. 'What does the public see?' he says. 'To take out all the intricacies of it, they see mass migration of people.' How do they see it? After offering anecdotes about Polish agricultural workers in the fields around his house, he accepts that really 'It's what Joe Public reads in the papers.' The power of Britain's right-wing media, and notably the glowering influence of Rupert Murdoch's *Sun* and Paul Dacre's *Daily Mail*, was and is immense, drip by drip, year by year.

Birkenhead is another Leave-voting coastal town with desperate economic and social conditions. Low wages and mistakes in benefit payments compel a section of the population into a daily quest just to stave off hunger. The Wirral Food Bank, with fifteen outlets across the district, is run by the recently retired Richard Roberts. Last year he and his team supplied over eleven thousand locals, 3538 of them children. 'The food bank is Birkenhead's fourth emergency service, saving those with nothing from catastrophe,' he says. The 100 tonnes distributed last year was mainly canned food – no answer to nutritional poverty.

It is in the Birkenheads and Weymouths of England that apprehension about immigration is keenest. But people are mostly at pains to explain they are not racist or xenophobic. The most active Birkenhead Remain campaigner in 2016, Collen Harrison, develops the point: 'You're not going to win here on economics and technical arguments. The problem is the EU is associated with a stagnant economy of small towns like this, and people are confusing austerity with an invasion of foreigners.' There was a moment in the 2016 campaign when Collen, on his street stall outside Birkenhead's M&S – about to close down – came face-to-face with the uglier side of nationalism. An ex-soldier aggressively heckled him as a 'traitor'. A few days later, Jo Cox was murdered by a man who gave his name at his trial as 'death to traitors, freedom for Britain'. After that, Collen refused to campaign alone and some enthusiastic students came over from Liverpool to help. But he still insists: 'The people here aren't racists; they just think opportunities have been taken away from them.'

In both Weymouth and Birkenhead the message was the same. Immigration was a kind of national emergency, a view that Nigel Farage propagated.

European DNA

The Brexit charge is that the European Union has become an overbearing political project threatening British sovereignty and values. Britain, so the story runs, is an exceptional country with an exceptional history, exceptional institutions and an exceptional destiny. For Europeans inured to political instability and bloodshed, supranational institutions are needed to keep the peace. These chosen British lands have no such need.

Like all caricatures, this story contains enough truth to be plausible. As the dominant part of an island to the west of the continent, England after 1066 was able to develop parliamentary government, religious toleration and common law without the periodic invasions that beset other parts of mainland Europe. It was not occupied by Napoleon or Hitler, or ravaged for decades by territorial-cum-religious war. It was first into the Industrial Revolution, and built the most extensive of the European empires on the basis of maritime prowess as an island nation. It was on the winning side in the twentieth century's two world wars. English, once spoken only in the Thames Valley, became the world language.

But there are limits to this account. It greatly overstates the uniqueness of English history, our differences with Europe, and our differences with the other nations of the British Isles. We have never been truly divorced from our continent. How could it be otherwise? England's violent record in Ireland, Scotland and Wales should disabuse anyone who thinks our history is distinctively peaceful – and our record in empire-building was of a piece. All the great currents that have shaped us – Roman, Saxon, Danish and Norman occupations, the Renaissance, the rise of Protestantism, the gains of overseas expansion, the concept of the nation-state, universal suffrage and the welfare state, industrialisation, the brutalities of early capitalism and the emergence of socialism – have shaped the rest of Europe too. The development has been symbiotic.

Thus, as we write in chapter 6, Magna Carta was part of a family of European settlements that fettered monarchical feudal rights across Europe. England's break with Rome under Henry VIII prefigured the cataclysm that overcame the Holy Roman Empire; England was part of the European state system established by the 1648 Treaty of Westphalia.

Sometimes, as with industrialisation, Britain was ahead of the pack, although we soon lost the advantage to Germany. Sometimes, as with votes for women in 1928 or laying the foundations of a welfare state before the First World War, we were well behind Scandinavia and even ex-colonies Australia and New Zealand. On the welfare state we took our cue from Bismarck. The Enlightenment was a pan-European movement. Indeed there is a powerful argument for viewing the British Industrial Revolution as a European event, given how many of the key inventions had origins in European thinking and in immigrants, many of them refugees compelled to seek better lives here.

The truth is that Britain has been integrating immigrants and sharing sovereignty for centuries. As urban centres grew and trade and cultural networks flourished, supported by revolutionary advances in technology from the three-masted sailing ship to the printing press to electrification to containerisation, these connections have woven Britain, Europe and the rest of the world closer together.

This interconnectedness has made cooperation more, not less, essential over time. Since 1834 Britain has signed more than thirteen thousand treaties and international conventions – a red-tape mountain – virtually all of which have diluted our notional sovereignty while advancing our national interest. The EU continues this process. The EU buildings that Johnson sees ominously 'looming over cobbled Brussels streets' are not representatives of some terrifying 'other': none of the EU's members have ambitions – whether public or cryptic – to submerge their nation into a federal superstate. There is no European army massing in Calais. The EU's buildings represent an often ticklish interdependence in which we Europeans devise solutions to shared problems – from environment to trade, from security to terrorism – that we could not have applied on our own. It is a construct for the future. Brexit is a step back to an imagined past that never existed.

European Britain

Even as England became a separate state from parts of the European mainland in the sixteenth century, engagement remained intense. Queen Elizabeth I, educated by disciples of the Dutch humanist Erasmus, spoke six European languages and regarded herself as a 'prince of Europe'. Resisting marriage advances by French and German princes lest they cramp her options, she was as deeply engaged as any of them in the culture and politics of the sixteenth-century European Reformation and Counter-Reformation.

William Shakespeare's Jaques said that 'All the world's a stage' but Europe was Shakespeare's actual stage – all of it, together with its history: Venice, Verona, Sicily, Denmark,

Athens, Rome, Paris, Vienna, Milan, Naples, Mantua, Cyprus, Bohemia, Illyria (Croatia), Navarre (Spain), Troy and Antioch (Turkey). And most exotic of all, the unnamed, heavenly Mediterranean isle of *The Tempest*, of which Caliban tells the shipwrecked Stephano: 'Be not afeard. The isle is full of noises, Sounds, and sweet airs that give delight and hurt not.'

Even Shakespeare's invocations of England are European. 'This royal throne of kings, this sceptred isle, This earth of majesty, this seat of Mars, This other Eden, demi-paradise ... set in a silver sea' – is conjured by John of Gaunt, 'Gaunt' being Ghent in Flanders, which includes Brussels. He is speaking in *Richard II*, aka Richard of Bordeaux. As for *King Lear*, one of the Bard's few plays set wholly in 'Britain', the cast list begins: 'Lear, King of Britain; the King of France; the Duke of Burgundy ... '

Political unions between England and mainland Europe continued long after Mary I, married to Philip II of Spain, was evicted from Calais in 1558. The Glorious Revolution of 1688 brought William of Orange (the Netherlands) to the English throne. After the death of the childless Queen Anne in 1714, the throne passed to her cousin George, Prince of Hanover, an Anglo-German union of crowns that continued until Queen Victoria's accession in 1837. Victoria promptly united with Saxe-Coburg in her marriage to Prince Albert. Of their nine children, one married the Emperor of Germany; others married into the royal families of Russia, Prussia, Denmark, Hesse, Schleswig-Holstein and Battenberg. Victoria's great-great-granddaughter, Elizabeth II – Elizabeth I of Scotland, which 'the Faerie Queene' did not rule – is cousin to the kings or queens of Norway, Denmark, Sweden, Spain and the Netherlands. Her husband, Prince Philip, is a prince of Greece and Denmark and son of a German princess. He once quipped to one of the authors that he was a 'European mongrel'.

So the monarchy is the most European of English institutions, just as it is the most Scottish and Welsh. It is nonetheless ambiguous, occupying a cultural borderland. For as well as her European relationships, the Queen continues to be head of state of Canada, Australia and New Zealand. She is also Head of the Commonwealth, a club of fifty-three mostly ex-colonies which still have strong cultural, educational, sporting and economic links to Britain despite the relative decline of the mother country. If those bonds are weakening, it is not because of the EU – it is because of Britain's fading economic and political relevance, despite the valiant efforts of the Royal Family.

A similar story of tension between England Alone and European Britain is told across England's intellectual, political, diplomatic, religious and cultural life. The two quintessential pieces of modern English music – the 'Hallelujah Chorus' and 'Nimrod', played on Remembrance Sunday – were respectively written by a German (Georg Friedrich Händel) and dedicated to a German, August Jaeger (one of Edward Elgar's closest musical friends). David Hockney was strongly influenced by Picasso, David Bowie's talent flowered in Berlin, George Orwell wrote in Paris and Catalonia. Isaac Newton was far more internationally famous than Shakespeare in his day, because he wrote for a European audience in Latin, when English was barely read on the European mainland. Only since the late eighteenth century have English language and culture held significant sway in mainland Europe. Even then, it took 150 years of intermittent revolution, turmoil and occupation for London to replace Paris as the capital of Europe.

By the late eighteenth century, Britain's leading scholars were writing in English, but no less engaged in Europe for their ideas and influence. Adam Smith, the father of modern economics, started writing *The Wealth of Nations* in Toulouse, while touring the continent as tutor to the Duke of Buccleuch. He met Voltaire in Geneva and David Hume in Paris, where his fellow Scot was Secretary of the British Embassy. Hume introduced him to all the great writers of the French Enlightenment. Smith even intended – his sudden death intervened – to dedicate his great book on the 'invisible hand' of the free market to François Quesnay, a French economist as well as physician to King Louis XV.

The Industrial Revolution arrived first in Britain not just because of unique British genius, or because we had abundant coal and running soft water, but due to the crucial interplay with the European Enlightenment. The leading economic historian Joel Mokyr argues that the quest for useful knowledge that defined the Industrial Revolution – the great inventors experimenting with new inventions and innovations like James Watt, Richard Arkwright and Josiah Wedgwood – was inspired by an Enlightenment seeking to open up the world to the force of reason. Inventors and thinkers alike converged on Britain, whose political institutions, tolerance and openness made it a European hub. As David Hume wrote: 'Notwithstanding the advanced state of our manufactures we daily adopt, in every art, the inventions and improvements of our neighbours.' Whether Leblanc's soda-making system, Jacquard's loom or De Girard's wet-spinning process, the British proved adept at absorbing European ideas from whatever source to reinforce their technological prowess and leadership.

The Industrial Revolution transformed not only British but also European societies and polities. Managing the convulsions and uncertainties associated with industrialisation led to common responses: while the details differed from place to place, social unrest allied to Enlightenment views of individualisation and human rights were a catalyst for democratisation, which in turn opened the door for redistribution and the extension of social and educational rights to the mass of the population. William Beveridge, godfather of the NHS and post-war welfare state, studied extensively the systems of compulsory social insurance for pensions and sickness which Bismarck had introduced into Germany in the 1880s. Beveridge wrote about them as a journalist at the Tory *Morning Post*. This work caught the eye of a thirty-three-year-old Winston Churchill, who in 1908 brought the twenty-nine-year-old Beveridge into the Board of Trade. A year later, Beveridge's ideas were central to the forty-six-year-old Lloyd George's famous People's Budget of 1909. It was the rise of a new pan-European generation.

England's self-styled Brexit historian Robert Tombs argued after the 2016 referendum that joining the European Union was 'an immense historic error' born of 'exaggerated fears of national decline and marginalisation [and] a vain attempt to be at the heart of Europe'. But his *The English and their*

History, published two years before the Brexit vote, when it looked as if it would go the other way, makes no such claim for English exceptionalism. Its rich tapestry of England's intense engagement and rapprochement with its neighbours more readily sustains an argument for British leadership in Europe than it justifies disengagement. 'England's successive incorporation into Great Britain, the United Kingdom, the empire, the European Community, and a multi-cultural global society added ever more layers of identity,' he declares. 'The past it seems is not dead; it is not even past.'

Churchill – from 'three great circles' to one

The greatest Briton, Winston Churchill, exemplifies the English European who never turned his back on the European mainland.

Churchill had an American mother and an imperial destiny from his boyhood at Harrow and Sandhurst, as a young officer on India's North-West Frontier and then a reporter in the South African War. Yet he was equally proud of being a descendant and biographer of the Duke of Marlborough, victor of Blenheim in league with Germans against the hegemonic *Roi Soleil*, Louis XIV.

And therein lies an episode of significance for the history of Europe. While visiting Marlborough's battlefields in Bavaria in 1932, Churchill nearly met Hitler. The Nazi leader, about to take power, had been due to meet Churchill at his hotel in Munich but – in a moment rich with symbolism – he cancelled at the last minute because Churchill had berated the Nazi leader's press secretary the night before about anti-Semitism. 'Why is your chief so violent about the Jews? ... What is the sense of being against a man simply because of his birth? How can any man help how he is born?', Churchill recalled saying. And the upshot: 'He must have repeated this to Hitler, because about noon the next day he came round with rather a serious air and said that the appointment could not take place.' Maybe the most fateful non-meeting in history.

Churchill never saw empire as a reason for British isolation from Europe. Faced by the ultimate crisis, he spurned Chamberlain's isolationist view of Czechoslovakia as 'a far-away country'. Instead he stood up to Hitler, offered the French an 'indissoluble union' to keep them in the war as Hitler's armies advanced on Paris in June 1940, refused to contemplate the armistice urged on him by his Foreign Secretary Lord Halifax after the fall of France, and pursued to the end a war to liberate Europe from 'the pestilence of Nazi tyranny'. But note for devotees of *Darkest Hour* and *Dunkirk*: Britain was never 'alone', and could not have triumphed had it been so. Even in its darkest hour Britain could call on its then vast empire, and within eighteen months on the Americans too. It also had a powerful defence industry, built up in the 1930s – as we recalled in chapter 1 – by methods that rejected laissez-faire.

Today's pro- and anti-Europeans quote different Churchill post-war speeches. 'We must build a kind of United States of Europe' is the classic federalist quote from his 1946 Zurich speech. 'We are with them, but not of them' is the classic anti-integration quote when he was prime minister for the second time in 1953. However, swapping quotes out of context is no substitute for understanding Churchill's thinking, which was consistently in favour of strong European engagement.

For Churchill – as for Attlee, his internationalist Labour counterpart – the issue of the 1940s was to combine European engagement, imperial power and global partnership with the United States. He set this out at length in his 'three great circles' speech at Llandudno in 1948. 'I almost wish I had a blackboard, I would make a picture for you,' he told Tory activists.

> The first circle for us is naturally the British Commonwealth and Empire. Then there is the English-speaking world in which we, Canada, and the other British Dominions and the United States play so important a part. And finally there is United Europe. These three majestic circles are co-existent and if they are linked together there is no force or combination which could overthrow them or even challenge them. ... We stand ... here in this Island at the centre of the seaways and perhaps of the airways also, we have the opportunity of joining them all together. [In doing so] we hold the key to opening a safe and happy future to humanity, and will gain for ourselves grati-tude and fame.

Churchill's approach was unambiguously to maximise British influence in all three circles, not to disengage. Seventy years after Llandudno, Britain has only one circle left intact – 'United Europe' – and it is implausible that Churchill would have favoured disengagement from that one. On the contrary, he would have seen British leadership of the EU as all the more imperative because it is now our principal circle of influence. He would have been equally resolute in support of NATO, being the legacy of his wartime alliance with the United States which still secures British security and influence, but it is inconceivable that he would have regarded this as a substitute for the EU.

The key point about Churchill's 1953 'with them but not of them' remark is that it was in the context of France and Germany debating the establishment of an integrated 'defence community' separate from the US, a stillborn precursor of the economic community that they went on to found in 1957. Churchill was not in principle against close military engagement with France and Germany, but in the context of the early 1950s he did not want to weaken the Anglo-American bedrock of NATO by supporting a speculative bid for a European army.

In the event, the French Parliament rejected the defence community, for reasons similar to Churchill's. However, on economic co-operation Churchill was consistently positive. 'We are prepared to consider, and if convinced to accept, the abrogation of national sovereignty, provided that we are satisfied with the conditions and the safeguards,' he said of the Schuman Plan in 1950. A year later he was more explicit in disowning isolationism: 'There are disadvantages and even dangers to us in standing aloof.' And after he left No. 10, he supported Macmillan's application to join the EU, having privately opposed Eden's ill-fated Suez expedition in 1956.

'In defeat, defiance' was another Churchill maxim. He never gave up the struggle to change public opinion and the Conservative Party to his way of thinking – even when threatened with deselection as Tory MP for Woodford in Essex, now Iain Duncan Smith's constituency, for opposing Chamberlain on his Munich agreement with Hitler to dismember Czechoslovakia.

Where the weather comes from

The Brexiter argument that Britain has outgrown the old continent has a long pedigree. Global Britain, descended from the 'blue water' tradition, assumes a future in which Britain escapes European geography, European engagement and European immigration. Out in that blue yonder, there are no risks, no power imbalances and no limitations on sovereignty.

This Global Britain, ludicrously branded 'Empire 2.0' by some Brexiters, is a piece of flimsy nonsense, particularly as our former empire is entirely self-governing, the Commonwealth is a club with no clout and there are no uncolonised continents besides the Antarctic ripe for exploitation. The reality is that British strategic thinking has always been – has always had to be – at least as European as global. European balance-of-power politics, so advancing our national interest, has been a central theme of our history. We resisted the emergence of Spain, then France and then Germany as would-be dominators of our continent by building countervailing alliances. We helped defend Europe against outside predators – the Turks in their time, and in the last century the Soviet Union. The crusades, misguided as they were,

were in their day quintessentially European. Britain built its overseas possessions in part to secure a better counterweight in Europe.

As Churchill said, Europe is 'where the weather comes from'. It is a Brexit fallacy that being out of the EU means being spared what happens in the EU and the Eurozone. Britain has an existential interest in what happens in Europe, as it always has. There is no hiding place in the Atlantic.

Today risks are mounting. As we argue in chapters 6 and 7, democracy is under threat worldwide, even in recently confident and progressive Western Europe and North America. Putin's Russia is behaving like the fascist regimes of the 1930s, backed by sophisticated raids from online troll factories. Citizens – and ominously younger voters in some European countries – are more and more willing to tolerate the subversion of democratic norms and express support for authoritarian alternatives.

Oleg Kalugin, former major general of the Committee for State Security (the KGB), has described sowing dissent as 'the heart and soul' of the Putin state:

> Not intelligence collection, but subversion: active measures to weaken the West, to drive wedges in the Western community alliances of all sorts, particularly NATO, to sow discord among allies, to weaken the United States in the eyes of the people of Europe, Asia, Africa, Latin America, and thus to prepare ground in case the war really occurs. To make America more vulnerable to the anger and distrust of other peoples.

Back in Weymouth, Captain Shakesby of UKIP is unruffled by Putin or European populism. He inhabits the cartoon world of British exceptionalism, and his main concern today is Mrs May's 'sell-out' of the referendum result. Brexit, uncorrupted, will be a success. 'It will work because the British people are resilient,' he says. Then, in full Dunkirk mode: 'In the Second World War, when we were down, we managed to pull through. The French couldn't hack it, the Netherlands couldn't hack it, the Belgians couldn't hack it. We would have done what Churchill said, fight them on the beaches. That's what nobody else ever does.' Of course Churchill did not actually do that – fighting on the beaches; and his whole statesmanship was to ensure that we did not have to either.

The MP for Captain Shakesby's South Dorset constituency is a Conservative who won the seat from New Labour in 2010. He too is a captain, one Captain Richard Grosvenor Plunkett-Ernle-Erle-Drax, educated at Harrow, then Sandhurst and the Coldstream Guards, grandson of Admiral Sir Reginald Drax and great-grandson of Lord Dunsany, second-oldest title in the peerage of Ireland. Captain Drax is quintessential governing class. At least six of his ancestors since the seventeenth century were MPs for Dorset or Gloucestershire. His home: the ancestral seat, Charborough House, Grade 1 listed, deer park and seven thousand acres. The grounds are open to the public twice a year, when the villagers of Sturminster Newton are admitted to sell tea and cakes.

Drax's view on Brexit? 'Resignation is the only honourable path' for MPs who won't accept it. Captain Drax is tribute to the Faragist takeover of the Tory Party. It is a party now indifferent to Britain's place in Europe and blind to the vital need for full engagement with our continent. Mouthing Churchillian rhetoric, while disowning the statecraft that underpinned it, is the lion without the roar.

4

Get real

Brexit is a hard-right project which rarely speaks its name, to hammer home the Thatcher revolution. Brexiters pretend that once outside the EU, the world becomes an economic Eden raining down free fruit. There are no hard decisions or trade-offs. Britain, long thwarted by its dalliance with the EU, can freely gorge. This is cynical dishonesty based on wilful ignorance. It is time to get real.

The modern trilemma

No country in today's world can enjoy democracy, global economic integration and untrammelled national sovereignty free of international organisations. It is fool's gold, because they are incompatible goals, unless the country concerned is willing to don the straitjacket of voluntarily doing all that global markets want – deregulation, small government, super-low taxes, a bias against trade unions, and minimal public health, education and welfare. Of course that is what most Brexit leaders privately long for, but it is not an expression of sovereignty but of subservience. What comes first are the needs of the world's multinationals and capital markets. That is where 'control' resides.

If you want to exercise democracy in a global economy, making genuine political choices, sovereignty has to be pooled, otherwise only two other options exist: sign up to whatever global markets demand, or systematically withdraw from global markets and engagement, to grow insular and poor. There is no third way outside the EU.

The genius of the EU, the product of the best of European civilisation, is that it comes as near as any institution in the world to allowing its democratic member states to manage the trilemma of reconciling sovereignty, democracy and reaping the benefits of global trade.

To promote effective trade, there has to be a mutual dropping of tariffs (taxes) on goods and services, a mutual recognition of each other's standards, and a willingness over time to regulate non-tariff barriers to trade – such as rules to protect the environment or employment standards. Without this it is simply a race to the bottom. Hence the democratic challenge. Non-tariff barriers to trade represent democratic choices that countries have made about what they value. They are especially important in services, which in today's advanced economies make up at least three-quarters of GDP. Countries have very different approaches to standards in, say, insurance, health, construction, engineering or education. A sovereign government can certainly overrule those democratically expressed preferences in order to cut a trade deal – but in so doing it abrogates democracy. For what that entails in practice, as already the preliminary skirmishes with the US have shown, is demands that Britain surrender its principled approach to regulations of food or health in return for further market access.

If it wants to cut 'quick and simple' trade deals with far more powerful countries like China and the US, Brexit Britain will have to betray a host of deeply held preferences among British voters – not, say, to eat chlorinated chicken, not to buy goods made by children, not to surrender personal data to Chinese and American social media companies. We will be wielding our sovereignty only to surrender it. In this respect the EU represents a triumph too little understood because too little explained. The EU *is* the modern solution to reconciling democracy, sovereignty and prosperity.

The genius of the EU

The EU's customs union, abolishing all internal tariffs and quotas between its twenty-eight member states, and imposing a common but low or zero tariff with all 'third countries' that trade with it, was the first step in the creation of today's European free-trade area. The next step was to reduce or eliminate all those non-tariff barriers to trade. This decisive second step was taken in the 1980s under Mrs Thatcher's leadership when the EU committed to create a 'single market'. To achieve this takes organisation, regulation and common standards – aka 'red tape'. But the prize is huge as the EU generates common standards on everything from packaging

requirements to product safety, so that there is no block to
goods and services moving from one country to another –
vastly boosting trade.

Trading standards are not bureaucratic inventions. They
reflect common concerns among European citizens about
safety, health and quality, that British people share and will
not readily give up in a 'deregulating' Brexit. The opinion-poll
evidence is overwhelming. There is solid public support for
EU standards on vehicle emissions, renewable energy, bankers' bonuses, consumer rights, limits to working hours and
conferring rights on temporary workers. Indeed the popular –
even populist – demand is to extend them.

British consumers may not know the detail of the REACH
regulations (Registration, Evaluation, Authorisation and
restriction of Chemicals) that EU chemical producers have
to follow to ensure product safety, or of EU requirements on
data privacy – but if British trade negotiators try to trash them
to appease the US or China, there will be uproar. They do
not represent the suffocating burden that right-wing Brexiters
inveigh against. Rather they exist to ensure that a maximum of
goods and services can flow across member-state borders with
probity and safety, and in keeping with standards that reflect
democratically expressed preferences. Infringements go to the
European Court, ensuring that the rules of the single market
are complied with.

Once a company complies with regulations in any one EU
country, it has the right to trade anywhere – so-called passporting rights. These have been particularly important for financial
services and the City of London: 5500 British-based financial

institutions enjoy such rights. Brexiters airily insist that the
same can be achieved by mutual recognition that the other's
standards are equivalent – 'equivalence' – but this is a paltry
fallback. It is highly bureaucratic and can only cover about a
third of financial services activities. Moreover even to achieve
this limited degree of access, the EU requires third countries –
Britain is set to become a third country – to shadow new EU
laws. In theory it might be the other way around, but in practice the EU bloc of 446 million people is not going to ditch its
standards to suit the UK with 63 million, which is the reason
why it was so sensible to pool sovereignty in the EU. Moreover
'equivalence' designations can be withdrawn by Brussels with
thirty days' notice. Passporting is also important to many
manufacturers. Airbus, the pan-European aviation manufacturer which directly and indirectly employs more than fifty
thousand people, is able freely to move parts around the EU
because it has passporting rights. It worries that its post-Brexit
capacity to organise its supply chain freely will disappear – as
do all UK-based manufacturers with EU supply chains from
car manufacturers to pharmaceutical companies.

These are fundamental trading freedoms. Such is the
volume of lorries leaving Dover each day that even a
two-minute check for customs processing would create a
seventeen-mile queue. A seven-minute check on every lorry
would create queues fifty miles long back to the M25. Non-EU
lorries in French ports have on average seven-minute waiting
times, so such concerns are very real. Britain's imports of fresh
food, mainly from the EU, run at around £22 billion a year; any
interruption or delays to its transit could make it inedible, with

the threat of a food crisis. The modern British economy needs frictionless trade with its close neighbours. All will disappear unless Britain remains in both the European customs union and single market.

The genius of the EU is that all these intense and growing flows of goods and services happen in a democratic framework. Every signatory to the EU is a democracy. The elected ministers of all EU states, on a basis of equality, meet regularly in the relevant European Council in Brussels to discuss their readiness to reach agreement on trade proposals put forward by the European Commission, itself appointed by elected governments. Negotiations for free-trade agreements between countries outside the EU framework can take years, and are then very hard to change. Negotiations between multiple countries have become virtually impossible, as proved by the last failed attempt by the World Trade Organization (WTO) to extend trade agreements – the abortive Doha round. By contrast the EU system is a permanent, ongoing and democratic negotiation, with members pre-agreeing that they will implement what has been agreed rather than obfuscate and stall – and with an effective process for change over time. As a further democratic backstop the directly elected European Parliament can block or seek to amend any measure. Every country has the opportunity to decide whether the gains from the new proposal offset any losses, so that any qualification to its sovereignty is premeditated and democratically validated.

This process takes time and involves protracted negotiation, but it is one by which the EU has created the deepest free trade area in the world – congruent with democracy and sovereignty. And here lies yet another Brexiter canard. Laws are not imposed by unelected bureaucrats in the European Commission, as they claim. Rather it is the Council of Ministers, made up of ministers from elected national governments, and the elected European Parliament that turn the Commission's draft propositions into law, or decline to do so. Moreover, the UK has rarely been outvoted. Between 2009 and 2015, it was on the winning side 87 per cent of the time, notwithstanding we were the member state most likely to vote against the majority. Some regulations – like the rules on the shape of bananas that attract such mockery – result from pressure from industry and international trade bodies for common standards, and have been accepted by all or most major trading nations. Scorn about the shape of fruit masked the reality: the UK was the principal architect of the world's most important rule-making body.

The Brussels effect

Because the EU is so effective and its market so large, its trading standards are rapidly becoming the global standards – the 'Brussels effect'. Foreign companies who want to produce at scale naturally adopt EU standards, because they are often the strictest. They know that if they adopt the strictest standard, they will be in compliance with laxer standards found in other large markets such as China and the US. This is cheaper and more convenient for companies than tailoring compliance systems for every different market. Many then lobby their governments to adopt the same standards. Without any coercion or formal agreements, suddenly the EU finds itself the global standard setter. Far from being a Brussels diktat, this amounts to EU soft power on a global scale, stopping an international race to the bottom. The EU is holding the line, creating a dynamic for excellence, a reality that left-wing critics of global capitalism fail to appreciate or worse, take for granted.

Anu Bradford of Columbia University spells out what it means:

> Few Americans are aware that EU regulations determine the makeup they apply in the morning, the cereal they eat for breakfast, the software they use on their computer, and the privacy settings they adjust on their Facebook page. And that's just before 8.30 am. The EU also sets the rules governing the interoffice phone directory they use to call a coworker. EU regulations dictate what kind of air conditioners Americans use to cool their homes and why their children no longer find soft plastic toys in their McDonald's Happy Meals.

American companies, knowing that to trade in the EU they will have to comply, readily do so because of the value of the business at stake. They choose to be EU-compliant because that will make them naturally compliant with laxer US regulation. Tellingly Facebook declared, in the wake of the crisis over its passing of data to Cambridge Analytica, that it will comply with the EU's General Data Protection Regulation, much tougher than those in the US on data privacy, as part of its efforts to restore confidence. The rest of the industry is following suit. Again, the EU is leading the way.

The EU's anti-trust and anti-monopoly powers are also becoming the global standard. American competition authorities may wave a bid through, but if the European Commission thinks it has anti-competitive implications within the EU it can block it. And if the merger can't happen in the EU, sheer economics means that it can't happen anywhere. When US aircraft giant Boeing bid for fellow US manufacturer McDonnell Douglas, the EU said it would only agree if Boeing dropped its exclusive supply arrangements with American airlines. It did so, opening up a big new market for European companies. Whether through fines on Microsoft or insistence that Google abide by European privacy standards, the EU has clout to achieve ends that British citizens totally endorse.

Brexiters damn EU regulation as burdensome and worthless. Here Johnson, Gove and Rees-Mogg sound just like those 'freedom-loving' Victorian industrialists who fought restrictions on child labour and limits on working hours as shackles on commercial enterprise, in opposition to Lord Shaftesbury. They have so little regard for the EU's achievement, so much libertarian distrust of the preferences and values that have created it, that they reject even a Brexit in which Britain continues to reflect these advantages through a deep free-trade agreement – so-called 'regulatory alignment'. This, they claim, would make Britain a 'vassal state'. Their real agenda, as we argue throughout this book, is the triumph of 'Thatcherism in one country'.

Global Britain – fool's gold

Brexiters claim that Global Britain, freed from the EU, can compensate for the loss of EU trade with 'quick and simple' deals with non-EU countries. This is pure fantasy, denying the truths of mathematics, geography, politics and economics.

For a start the World Trade Organization is not the all-powerful fairy godmother of free trade portrayed by the Brexit innocents. It is no substitute for the EU. Its founders did not empower it to be the world free-trade policeman. Its task and powers are more modest. Its mandate and focus are tariffs, which in any case have fallen everywhere; for example the EU's trade-weighted tariff on imports from other members of the WTO, allegedly strangling British trade, is a mere 2.8 per cent.

Over and above the rates at which tariffs are set, the WTO tries to ensure they are non-discriminatory, so that countries apply the same tariff to all importers. It has powers to adjudicate between disputes – but crucially, unlike the EU, no powers of enforcement. It is only as effective as its members' willingness to abide by its rules and judgements within the limited scope of trade it oversees, having only the power that its signatories assign. It cannot compel a member state to lift what it rules as restrictive trade measures, even when it authorises sanctions against it – which in any case are non-retrospective. Famously the EU, insisting that its ban on genetically modified food imports represents the preferences of its member states, refuses to lift its ban on American GMO food and hormone-treated beef, despite the WTO's judgement that it must do so 'without delay'. If the US cannot get the EU to comply with a WTO trade ruling, Britain's efforts will be weaker still. The WTO has only feeble leverage over non-tariff barriers to trade, and virtually none over services – the key areas of concern to British exporters.

Worse, the WTO is getting even weaker. The Doha round of free-trade talks, launched in 2001 to address non-tariff barriers to trade and to promote cross-border trade in services, has been suspended, having made zero progress. There is not even agreement as to whether the round is over. Unity has collapsed into sixteen formal coalitions and numerous informal alliances inside the WTO – each overlapping in complex, unpredictable ways. The idea that they are suddenly going to drop their arguments and come together as a force for free trade, urged on through the leadership of a 'Global Britain' outside the EU is twaddle. On top of that, China and the US are actively signalling their unwillingness to play by WTO rules. China has been particularly slow in moving towards acceding to the WTO Government Procurement Agreement (GPA), while the US has failed to agree judicial appointments to the WTO's judicial panels, effectively neutering it. Worse, Trump now proposes 25 per cent tariffs on imported steel, not in concert with others – as the toothless WTO requires – but unilaterally. The world has taken a step towards a trade war, with the WTO helpless to intervene. To rely on the WTO alone as our guarantor of global market access, as Rees-Mogg's European Research Group argue, would send a British lamb to an ugly slaughter.

Make-believe proliferates in the Brexit wonderland. Britain

should pivot from sclerotic Europe to dynamic Asia, runs the Brexit refrain. False. The growth of Asian and other emergent economies cannot continue at the same pace as they grow richer: indeed, the slowdown is already happening. The lesson of the last fifty years is that it is comparatively easy to grow quickly from being a low-income country to a middle-income one – but growing beyond to match the productivity and riches of the advanced industrialised West is a long trek. Shifting workers from agriculture to industry, exporting cheap manufactures and importing foreign technology have quick results: but the next phase requires diversifying the economy so that it has its own innovative capability. This is much harder, and few countries have managed it. Of 101 middle-income economies in 1960, only thirteen had become high-income by 2008.

The EU's record on trade is exceptionally strong. Over the last decade each percentage point increase in GDP growth in Europe is associated with proportionately more trade. And over the last two years it is 'sclerotic' Europe that has contributed virtually as much, so the IMF calculates, to the growth of global goods imports as China and the US combined. Europe is at last overcoming the financial crisis of 2008/9, resuming growth within the EU and external trade. EU membership does not stop German, Italian and French exporters profiting from Asian markets; it is the weakness of British exports that holds us back, not the EU – in particular our incapacity to produce high-value manufactured goods. Thus EU–India trade has more than tripled since 2000, but UK–India trade has stagnated despite the Commonwealth. The UK share of EU exports to India has fallen from 29 per cent to 10 per cent over the same period. It is not the EU stopping Britain from being a global trading power. It is our lack of economic strength.

Mathematics and geography also matter. The economic model used by Brexit economist Patrick Minford assumes that Australia, in the world of container transport, is as near as France, and that all goods and services are identical in quality – the only arbiter is price. Minford's assumptions and model are plain ludicrous. Every study on trade shows that distance matters; typically as distance doubles, trade halves. Face-to-face contact counts enormously, especially in services. In goods, it is the global supply chain that dictates 80 per cent of all trade – and manufacturers value their suppliers' proximity because it means greater agility in flexing the supplies of goods. The nearer a supplier, the easier to adjust any order up and down. You can share language, culture, law and have low border barriers: but you cannot abolish distance, even with computerisation of logistics and the big container, not least when Europe's principal container port is Rotterdam. Proximity is especially important for smaller companies seeking to export: for them, the EU is usually their first market abroad, and only if successful do they expand to markets beyond. Big or small, you do more business with your neighbours – and that becomes a launch pad for more distant ambitions. This is as basic as the law of gravity.

Most of the UK's too modest exporting success has depended vitally on the EU. The single market has created some great British companies. The rise of Vodafone, one of the few British companies to have grown to global standing in the last twenty-five years, was made possible by the EU, which set European mobile phone technology standards that in the 1990s became the global standard over the US's. Successive EU competition commissioners insisted that the EU-wide telecoms market was opened up to competition to private mobile phone operators. Vodafone's daring bid for the German mobile company Mannesmann in 2000, which as an EU company could not be stopped by the German government, gave it the foothold it needed in Germany, now its largest European national business. Vodafone has 20 million customers in Britain – but another 100 million in the rest of the EU. Its European base, and its possession of the global standard, allowed Vodafone to power its way into the Indian and Chinese markets where it has 850 million customers. Vodafone is an awesome British success story, responsible for one pound of every eight pounds of dividends paid in the London stock market.

'Today it is "European", not "British", models of regulation and policymaking which are studied by our counterparts in the US, India, China and Brazil,' declares Vodafone. 'They are interested not in what Britain might do, but in what Europe might do.' Brexit ensures that its success can never be repeated.

There is also the simple question of mathematics – not Johnson, Gove and Rees-Mogg's strong suit (Classics, English and History degrees respectively). A trade boom in new markets, from leaving the EU, is a mathematical impossibility. Theresa May recognised as much in her pre-2016 referendum speech making the case for staying in the EU. 'We export more to Ireland than to China, twice as much to Belgium as to India, and nearly three times as much to Sweden as to Brazil,' she said. 'It is not realistic to think we could replace European trade with these new markets.' Mrs May studied geography: she clearly understands distance.

Trade with China would have to increase ten times to get anywhere near the levels the UK enjoys with the EU. Nor are Liam Fox's much-vaunted free-trade agreements (FTAs) going to come to the rescue. Concluding FTAs with Brazil, Russia, India and China combined would boost UK trade just over 2 per cent, while concluding FTAs with all the Anglophone countries – USA, Canada, Australia and New Zealand – would result in a long-term increase in total UK trade of less than 3 per cent. Meanwhile our trade with Europe will suffer, because as Theresa May admitted in a more recent speech (February 2018), the unavoidable price of Brexit is 'less market access' to Europe. It is an understatement. If Britain secures a preferential trade agreement with the EU as she hopes – but to which her hard Brexiters are opposed – trade in goods will fall by 38 per cent, says the World Bank. With no deal, trade falls 50 per cent. Service trade would fall even further: by 50 per cent, and 62 per cent with no deal. There is no way that trade deals with Sri Lanka, Gabon and Chile are going to offset these losses.

Crucially, Britain's international competitive advantage is not in goods but in services, notoriously hard to advance in trade deals because the main barriers to service trade today are not customs tariffs, but ongoing and detailed non-tariff rules on acceptable and professional practice in fields like insurance and broadcasting. If China and the US are hostile to opening up their markets in goods, they are doubly so in

services. Services, apart from the vexed questions of standards and strategic importance, are intimately intertwined
with movement of people – it is people who support sophisticated service delivery, some of whom need to work and
live locally – a proposition unlikely to appeal to the Trump
administration, given its hardline stance on immigration.
Meanwhile all but a few Chinese banks, insurance companies
and funds remain fully or partly state-owned, central as they
are to the Chinese Communist Party's ability to control the
economy and society. Any liberalisation will be glacial and at
the very margins.

The EU's internal market in services may be work in
progress, but by international standards it is phenomenal –
because of the high levels of integration on market and
professional rules, achieved through the very European process, regulation and law to which the Brexiters object as a
matter of ideology. The UK's services trade with Europe has
more than doubled as a result. No such prospect awaits 'Global
Britain'. For all these reasons the former chief official in the
Department of International Trade, Sir Martin Donnelly,
damns Brexit: 'It is rejecting a three-course meal now for the
promise of a packet of crisps in the future!'

Unfree trade

A key Brexit fallacy concerns the whole concept of free trade.
For all the utopian rhetoric, free trade has always been desperately difficult to achieve between nations, and is usually
imposed by strong powers on weak. Britain's conversion

to free trade in the nineteenth century, to which Brexiters look back so fondly, was based on a hard-headed calculus of where national advantage lay. As the world's leading industrial power, from the 1820s Britain progressively lowered tariffs on imported food and raw materials in order to export more valuable manufactured goods aggressively to the lesser powers it bullied, either by conquest as in the case of India or by gunboat diplomacy in China.

Even Victorian Britain was much less open to trade than contemporary Britain has been inside the EU. Trade openness (total imports and exports as a share of economic output) has been more than twice as large on average during British membership of the EU as at the peak of the British Empire between 1830 and 1913. Governments, constantly lobbied by business and consumer groups, are keenly aware that trade throws up winners and losers, and they do their utmost to protect potential losers. What no one does is lower their tariffs – and non-tariff barriers – unilaterally, as in Jacob Rees-Mogg and Patrick Minford's wonderland. It is fanciful to believe that if our producers face tariffs from both the EU and other countries with whom we used to have preferential access because of EU Free Trade Agreements, there will be no impact on our exports.

These Brexit assumptions are absurd: garbage in, garbage out. Because the EU's external tariffs are already quite low or zero, dropping them would have minimal impact on prices. One estimate suggests that abolition of all tariffs would reduce consumer prices by, at most, between 0.7 and 1.2 per cent. And this estimate excludes the cost on those large parts of

British agriculture and manufacturing that would suffer by slashing tariffs across the board. Then there will be the costs of up to £27 billion, on one estimate, as British companies establish operations within the EU so as to be inside the single market and customs union, vital in sectors like financial services, cars, chemicals, consumer goods and food, to avoid the common external tariff. To cap it all, Britain would immediately surrender any bargaining power. Such a policy would be devastatingly self-defeating.

Trade is linked indissolubly to power. Both the US and China have strong anti-free trade traditions and policies. US founding father Alexander Hamilton believed in trade protection. So did the founder of the modern Chinese economy, Deng Xiao Ping. Donald Trump's preaching of America First has a long pedigree: the US routinely imposes punitive tariffs on imports that are considered high by international standards – whether it is on Japanese supercomputers or Chinese cold-rolled flat steel.

Trump is just the latest US agent of a protectionist reflex hardwired into both the culture and bureaucratic routines of the US state. Farmers in particular wield enormous power on Capitol Hill, particularly in the Senate, due to the over-representation of small farm-dominated states. In any trade deal the US has to deliver to its farmers, who operate on an industrial scale with standards much lower than those in Britain and Europe. John Gummer, a former Tory Environment Secretary, observes that 'the US has to chlorinate its chickens because it does not have high animal welfare standards, and unless you chlorinate them you have even more food-borne disease than America has now. It has at least four times the food-borne diseases we have in Europe. This is no passing comment: it is a fundamental issue of the health of the British people.'

Trump believes in a series of asymmetric America First trade deals; his officials have privately declared that the UK is 'on the ropes' and that the task ahead is to pick us off. British hopes that we could simply score out the words EU and substitute UK in an Open Skies deal with the US have already been dashed. The US requires foreign airlines to which it accords landing rights at US airports to be majority owned by the country with whom it has struck the agreement: but British Airways (now half Spanish owned thanks to the EU single market) and Virgin Atlantic do not meet the terms – and the US has refused to budge. Lack of agreement would hand enormous transatlantic airline traffic to US companies, grievously damaging British Airways and Virgin. This is why Theresa May has already changed tack and is now hoping to stay in EU aviation arrangements post-Brexit. The US is out to get what it can, and the power imbalance is stark.

China is no different. Its opening to the world since 1978 has been orchestrated so that China has access to global markets more freely than the world has access to its markets – justifying this as essential to its economic development. China is in constant search for joint ventures with advanced Western countries, obliging its trading partners and inward investors to transfer their technology. In China the joke is that R and D stands for 'Rob and Duplicate'. It is increasingly difficult for foreign companies to do business there; Beijing's 'Made in China 2025' industrial policy aims to increase 'indigenous innovation' and self-reliance. Under President Xi that approach is intensifying, with China growing its new digital giants and effectively keeping Facebook, Google and other US high-tech companies out of China. Economic nationalism is China's key foreign policy.

As for Brexit euphoria that Britain will be free from the European Court by going global, China has made it clear that all trade disputes involving its $1 trillion 'Belt and Road' programme to boost trade are to be settled in Chinese courts. The recently amended Chinese constitution replaces a commitment to the rule of law in favour of the Communist Party's right to use the 'law to rule'. As Switzerland discovered, an equitable free-trade agreement with China without the clout of the EU behind us is as likely as life on Mars. While Switzerland had to open its markets immediately to China, the Chinese only agreed to do the same for the Swiss over fifteen years.

One of Brexit's Great Lies is that the EU is poor at trade deals. Endless repetition does not make this true. In fact, the EU has an enviable record on trade negotiations. It has 750 international agreements with over sixty countries – much more extensive than either China or the US. It deploys clout that Britain alone – any UK-sized country alone – cannot muster. South Korea, for example, had to accept that its car-emission standards would shadow those of EU manufacturers, which has been vital to boosting British car exports to Seoul since the agreement came into force in 2010. The EU can deploy that clout in trade negotiations with China.

The EU is the global trade hotspot, with the densest network of cross-border supply chains and trade anywhere. Despite Brexit black propaganda, the sectors of the European economy where trade is most intense and competition most fierce are now at the global frontiers of technology and productivity. The EU was hard hit by the financial crisis, but the economies of Europe are now mounting an interconnected recovery. The EU is emerging as the global standard setter, and the force for keeping not only its own markets open, but other people's. The UK exerted a powerful influence on all these achievements, and is a major beneficiary. Yet in a bizarre though classic Brexit back-flip we are now proposing to leave, rejecting our own achievements over four decades. It is a monumental act of self-harm. Why commit it? The only rational argument is the necessity to respond to public concern about immigration, where again we need to get real.

Britain shapes its migrants

Both authors, like virtually all other Brits, are descended from immigrants. Andrew's father was a Greek Cypriot fleeing from conflict in Cyprus in the late 1950s, while Will's family can be traced back to the Danish invasions before the Norman conquest. Everybody in Britain will have similar stories to tell – some of us from families arriving earlier than others, but all of us having roots elsewhere, mostly in Europe. Britain has grown over centuries by assimilating newcomers, while sustaining generation by generation a shared sense of nationhood. It is a constant national evolution.

Today's British would find what was going on in the heads of their seventeenth- or eighteenth-century forebears very foreign – their unquestioning belief in heaven and hell, their superstitions, their attitude to gender and sexuality. Yet there would be elements we would understand – humanity's foibles captured in Shakespeare's plays or the trials of love celebrated by John Donne. As we saw in chapter 3, 'Britishness' has strong foundations, yet is a house in permanent construction and reconstruction. The children of immigrants quickly become British.

Britain shapes its migrants far more than migration shapes Britain. It takes confidence to recognise this essential truth. People are rightly proud and protective of where they live, and rapid and large-scale immigration is profoundly unsettling. It seems more obvious that immigrants are benefiting from coming to Britain and that the traffic is one-way. However, assimilation should be more explicit. London mayor Sadiq Khan, the most prominent Muslim leader in the country, expresses it this way:

People employed in public-sector jobs in London should speak English. Our public institutions should promote our common values and laws. We need to ensure our housing and planning laws mean we design and build integrated communities and institutions where neighbours have real reasons to come together. We should create the right conditions for new migrants to integrate fully, and we should be clear about our values and our expectations of them.

As Birkenhead's Collen Harrison said, Birkenhead's wariness of immigration is not rooted in racism, but rather in misgivings that it will make hard lives even harder. Survey evidence shows that even white UKIP voters, once aware that immigrants are genuinely assimilating, playing by the rules and contributing to British society, become much less concerned about immigration. Attitudes are not set in stone.

If Britain is to sustain its membership of the EU, there has to be a new settlement. People need to believe that Britain does indeed shape its migrants, and that public services and job opportunities for native British are not suffering.

Government must dramatically overhaul our training system, as set out in chapter 5. It is simply unacceptable that so many of our young are so ill-educated and poorly trained compared with East Europeans. Nor can we allow so much exploitation of East Europeans where they undercut British workers. Britain should enforce domestic and EU regulations on wages and standards. The lassitude and lack of will on enforcement cannot continue. Employment in public organisations like the NHS should give priority to UK nationals, as permitted under EU law.

ID cards should – urgently – be introduced as proposed by the Labour government in the 2000s, but defeated by Tory and Lib Dem opposition led by David Davis, on the skewed argument that they infringe civil liberties. Virtually every other European state has ID cards to stop illegal working and illicit access to public services, while also enabling the collection of proper data on those entering, leaving and present in the country. Any user of the Spanish healthcare system, for example, has to register with the social security authorities and show an ID card, while any resident of Germany, will be familiar with multiplicity of requirements to register and show evidence of entitlements. While dismantling sensible plans for ID cards, the Cameron government led by Home Secretary Theresa May started hounding perfectly legal immigrants to Britain. Had ID cards been in operation, there would have been no Windrush scandal.

Because of the absence of ID cards, immigration statistics in Britain, the source of so much political controversy, are slapdash. They are based on almost random surveys of passengers at ports and airports. Passports are no substitute for measurement when so many have multiple citizenship and travel, perfectly legally, on different documents. Without a robust system to track whether immigrants have returned home – especially students who constitute half the numbers and who irrationally are counted as immigrants even though their intended stay is guaranteed to be temporary – the immigration system lacks credible border controls because the government simply does not know who is in the country. This is nothing to do with the EU – everything to do with the UK.

Better to have ID cards than to leave the EU. Britain cannot allow distrust of immigration to morph into racism solely because it cannot assure its citizens that it knows about migrants entering and leaving the country and can regulate their access to work and public services on a proper legal basis.

The Cameron government compounded this first-order mistake of halting ID cards by abolishing the Migration

Impact Fund as soon as it came to power in 2010. This fund helped local authorities whose public services were under pressure from immigration. Six years later a pale imitation has been relaunched as the 'Controlling Migration Fund'. The resources provided are a pittance – £140 million over the four years from 2016 to 2020. Funding for areas with high immigrant numbers needs to be massively boosted, channelling funds into the NHS, schools, housing and local services on objective measures – and widely publicised so that citizens know that there is a determined and long-term response in operation.

EU citizens' right to enter the country and claim benefits should be properly regulated within EU law. If immigrants have not found a job within one hundred days they should be required to leave, as in Belgium. Entitlements for benefits should follow a national insurance contribution record of twelve months. And within the EU Britain should seek to negotiate an arrangement akin to the 'emergency brake' that David Cameron failed to negotiate before the 2016 referendum. EU workers would retain the right to work in Britain, but the government should have the power to restrict entry to those with a prior job offer, if numbers are too high on an agreed basis. This is essential for the long-term sustainability of migration across Europe not just in Britain.

It is time to get real.

5

Stakeholder capitalism and the new social contract

Brexit has forced a witching hour in British capitalism and our social contract. Both have been found wanting. Fundamental reform is now urgent. Social justice requires that every citizen in our islands should be confident of decent minimum living standards, comprehensive public services and the opportunity to make the best of their life, wherever they are born and live.

The building blocks of Brexit-Thatcherism are the beliefs, expedient for those doing well, that 'free' markets self-organise for the common good and that 'self-reliant' individuals should 'stand on their own two feet' in all circumstances. According to this neoliberal doctrine less government is necessarily better government, including withdrawal from the EU, and social justice is not a responsibility of the state. Margaret Thatcher's most notorious – and revealing – maxim was her insistence that 'there is no such thing as society'. Her followers see no need for a better social contract.

This laissez-faire ideology is poison at the heart of British politics. Brexit and austerity are its latest and most dangerous manifestations. We need the antidote: a new social contract based on stakeholder capitalism, offering fair shares and decent opportunities across society and across the country.

A new tune

Social justice and prosperity do not emerge spontaneously from self-organising markets and individualism. Any vestigial claim that they do was finally laid to rest by the cataclysm of the financial crisis in 2007/8, and the continuing failure of British companies – with honourable exceptions – to grasp the opportunities afforded by globalisation and new technologies.

Most of the British economy is populated by indifferently or poorly performing firms which cannot offer good wages, jobs or prospects because they themselves are so weak, even while those who run them are rewarded extravagantly. This weakens the national economy and breeds deep inequalities. There are far too few good companies and good jobs in modern Britain and Brexit – a protest against poverty and neglect – is a consequence.

John Maynard Keynes, writing nearly a hundred years ago, foretold the end of laissez-faire in his time: 'We do not dance even yet to a new tune. But a change is in the air.' Keynes and William Beveridge, with his wartime report on social insurance, laid the ethical foundation for the great Attlee government of 1945. Attlee's creation of the National Health Service, the welfare state and its commitment to full employment all took place within an avowedly internationalist setting of the United Nations, NATO, the World Bank and the International Labour Organization.

The Keynesian tune played on for a generation until, after a deep crisis of the state in its relations with the trade unions in the 1970s, Thatcher took charge. A highly organised and adroit faction of the Conservative Party seized its moment to change the music back to pre-Keynesian laissez-faire. 'Privatisation and the strong state' was its mantra, but it was a state strong mainly in facing down organised labour and redistributing wealth and opportunity to the already advantaged. The role of trade unions was replaced with a labour market based on disempowering individual workers.

In 1942 Beveridge famously declared war on the 'five giants' of Squalor, Ignorance, Want, Idleness and Disease. After forty years of laissez-faire, those evils have returned in the form of what GPs call 'shit life syndrome': low or non-existent skills, poverty, the futility of many working lives, and a mental health epidemic. Too many adults and children are hurting badly, with neither help nor hope. To defeat the 'five giants' we need a 2020 version of the ideas and practical imagination of Keynes, Beveridge and Attlee.

For all the self-serving bromides about the success of Britain's modern economy, the everyday truth is that much of British capitalism performs badly. There are too few great companies and too few sectors or industries where Britain can claim world leadership. This is especially resonant as we write in the spring of 2018 with a succession of corporate relocations to the European mainland and the automotive and aerospace GKN, the UK's third-biggest engineering company, set to be dismembered after a bitterly contested takeover won only through the votes of short-term hedge funds and arbitrageurs while the government wrung its hands and did nothing to intervene.

Melrose, the company taking over GKN and its fifty-seven thousand employees, is run by Christopher Miller, a protégé of Lord Hanson, the 1980s asset stripper, close to Thatcher, who dismembered much of British industry in complex financial transactions so that he and his financier clients could get rich quick. The stakeholders involved count for nothing. The City financiers who devise these financially engineered takeovers call it 'value creation'; in reality, it is value extraction leading to value demolition. Melrose will sell off large parts of GKN; what's left will be run to the ground to generate the cash to pay the huge debts incurred in the takeover. Hanson in the 1980s; Melrose in the 2010s: second-generation Thatcherism.

Britain has a few big companies, many small ones, but a sparse middle ground. Our medium-sized business sector – what in Germany is called the *Mittelstand*, the bedrock of its 'social market economy' – is small because of cultural and financial short-termism, and the lack of public institutions to support its growth. In particular, the UK has no indigenous high-tech companies of any size. Only one high-tech company – Sage – is represented in the *Financial Times* index of top 100 UK companies. The Cambridge-based semiconductor and software giant ARM, the only other high-tech company to feature in the index until 2016, was taken over opportunistically in the aftermath of the Brexit referendum by Japan's SoftBank. It is the same story with a cluster of smaller Cambridge high-tech companies with equally promising prospects, whose owners sold out as soon as they could amass personal fortunes.

This matters. A great economy requires a critical mass of thriving companies based and largely owned in the UK and proud of their roots, which invest and innovate, setting the benchmark and pace for productivity growth, good wages and social mobility. Britain's failure to grow enough good companies manifests itself in a lack of good jobs and skills and a dwindling belief that tomorrow will be better than today. The UK's hundred biggest companies give work to an average eight thousand smaller firms in their supply chain. They paid £83 billion of taxes in 2017 – 13 per cent of all government receipts. But there is no 'challenger' group of strong and growing companies behind them, offering employment and paying fair taxes in every part of the country.

Furthermore, companies large and small are disproportionately clustered in London and the south-east of England, even adjusting for population. This too has to change. National economic renewal depends upon a growing population of innovative companies in all parts of Britain, plus systems for diffusing innovation and best-practice approaches to productivity into their supply chains and *Mittelstand*.

This is a propitious moment to build stakeholder capitalism. New technologies offer immense possibilities. Ever since the European Enlightenment, captured in the German philosopher Immanuel Kant's injunction 'Dare to know, have the courage to know your own reason', the pace of innovation and invention has quickened. First it was the steam engine, to be succeeded by petrol engines, computers and electricity amongst others. The twenty-first century promises further extraordinary advance, which needs to be deployed in forging new and better companies.

Digitisation, still in its infancy, is set to be as transformational as steam and computing, disrupting existing business models with bewildering speed and reach. No human activity will be left untouched by the translation of the physical into digital data. Machines that process data ultra-fast are opening up new horizons from artificial intelligence to new materials and medical treatments. Jobs that involve routines that machines can learn will be rapidly displaced, from diagnosing patients to writing mortgage contracts, from inserting parts on an assembly line to driving lorries.

Alarmism that digitalisation will lead to a net loss of jobs is as misplaced as fears that power-looms in the nineteenth century and computers in the twentieth would do the same. Certainly the transition needs to be carefully managed, but alongside the jobs and companies created by new technologies there is a steadily rising demand for people to work in jobs involving face–to-face contact and human interaction – caring, teaching, coaching, nursing, hospitality. The challenge is to promote great British companies in all these areas, sustaining jobs with decent pay and employment rights. This will only happen if we dance to a new Keynesian tune of stakeholder capitalism.

The Cambridge economy

The first step needed is the boldest: to recognise that the market will not – because it literally cannot – self-organise to deliver prosperity and fairness. For many business leaders and in the City this is, as Keynes wrote in his attack on laissez-faire in his day, as difficult but critical a proposition for them to hear as explaining Darwin's *Origin of Species* to a Victorian bishop.

Once this Rubicon is crossed, a new world opens up.

The next step is to require companies to define their intrinsic social purpose as creating long-term value, to repel the Lord Hansons. This requires the creation of a supportive environment of 'stakeholder capitalism' in law, procurement, employment rights and public support for innovation, research, investment, training and regional development.

In the US it is well documented that for all the adulation of the free market, most of the technologies deployed commercially by Apple in the iPhone were pioneered, funded and promoted by the US Department of Defense and other public research agencies. In the UK, frontier research in Rolls-Royce's aero-engines and key advances in GlaxoSmithKline's drug capabilities, including path-breaking cancer treatments, were substantially funded by the government or procured at first by the NHS. Yet so weak is the common understanding of the way that companies depend on the state that many a swashbuckling chief executive does not hesitate to resort to tax avoidance and accountancy scams. It is the task of the state, as the guardian of the public, to see that their obligations are strictly defined and honoured.

Worldwide there are beacons of stakeholder capitalism to admire, particularly in Europe, often with university 'brain hubs' at their core. Britain boasts the best university system in the world for an economy of its size. To create brain hubs, the universities involved don't have to be global leaders like Oxford and Cambridge, or like Stanford and MIT in the US – although the catalytic impact is obvious in all four cases. Eindhoven's technical university in Holland has become a vibrant hub in collaboration with Phillips. Dresden's Max Planck Institute in Silicon Saxony became one of Germany's leading nodes of growth once freed from communist East Germany twenty-five years ago. London, with its forty higher educational institutions and four hundred thousand students, is one giant brain hub. Bristol, Leeds and Brighton owe much of their vitality and spin-out enterprises to their mostly young graduates.

To encourage more 'brain hub' clusters in the UK requires a bold assertion of what the political economist Mariana Mazzucato calls 'the entrepreneurial state' – a state that backs research and innovation and promotes companies and public services that apply them. Devolution to cities and regions is vital to building new regional powerhouses, as proposed in chapter 6. Equally essential is the long-term momentum imparted by substantive, targeted public investment. London's new east–west underground Elizabeth Line, which will add 10 per cent to the capital's commuter rail capacity and create new cities out of Slough and Maidenhead, and the new HS2 high-speed line from London to the North, which trebles rail capacity and will bring Birmingham, Manchester and Leeds within hourly travelling distance of London, are tributes to the entrepreneurial state. The more ambitious and genuinely 'smart' projects the entrepreneurial state can identify and fund – from agriculture to space and advanced materials – the better for Britain.

Thatcherite faith that 'the market' always knows best, and that state activity to promote entrepreneurialism is a futile task of 'picking winners', is imploding. The truth about the 1970s, when crisis engulfed many once-great companies like Rolls-Royce and British Leyland, is not that an arrogant state gambled on 'picking winners', but rather that failing companies 'picked the state'. Even then, the state as often succeeded (Rolls-Royce) as it failed (BL). In truth, the public sector fails and succeeds about as often as the private sector. Like every other part of society, the state should constantly seek to do its job better, but not abdicate lest it fail.

Another free-market canard is that state entrepreneurialism can only be justified if there is proven 'market failure', in the belief that the great god laissez-faire is generally all-seeing and all-wise. The more rational Keynesian presumption – central to stakeholder capitalism – is that markets are, like all human institutions, constantly and inherently unstable. This is not an argument against markets, but an argument against fetishising unregulated markets. Their default mode is violent, over-exaggerated mood shifts. They need to be designed, overseen and equipped to deliver the public good. So entrenched is laissez-faire that even where the state acts entrepreneurially it pretends not to do so. Thus the government has created a network of 'catapult' centres – originally modelled on Germany's successful business research initiatives, the Fraunhofer Institutes – with a mission to stimulate new technologies, start-ups and scale-ups. But for fear of the great god laissez-faire Whitehall is now reverting to micro-managing thinly spread grants so that too little can be ventured.

Stakeholder capitalism does not obsess about market failure; it obsesses about value creation, good companies and good jobs. It recognises that some state-sponsored failures are inevitable in trying to create business at the technological and scientific frontier. The state should give the catapults their autonomy, and the confidence to help create successful enterprises.

So high is the number of low-performing firms in the UK that just modest improvement among this long tail will yield dramatic returns. To achieve this requires systematic company mentoring so that good firms can help laggards, for example in becoming exporters. There is also scope for radical gains in productivity in the expanding world of 'face-to-face' companies, in services ranging from hospitals to supermarkets, which make up some two-fifths of all British jobs but where productivity is poor. Retail and hospitality alone comprise 23 per cent of the British economy, but account for 30 per cent of our productivity gap compared with France and Germany because of poor training, management and investment.

Most British companies, even in the social economy with its strong public and social character, have little overt commitment to public and social goals. Shabbily and myopically, there is a band of employers who typically set out to minimise wage costs by systematically creating zero-hours, short-term and nil-benefits forms of employment. The laissez-faire assumption is that there is an intrinsic conflict between fair employment and delivering returns to shareholders or taxpayers. This is self-serving nonsense peddled by a dominant faction in the City – lawyers, consultants, fund managers, advisers and their intellectual acolytes – who feast on the lush fees and commissions of the existing system. Rather the legal presumption in employment law should be that employees are members of the firm with standard stakeholder rights offering the full range of attendant employment benefits together with appropriate job security. The non-standard employment contract should be the exception rather than the new normal.

Value in businesses is created by stakeholder capitalism properly balancing investors, employees, customers, suppliers and the public. Evidence assembled by the Big Innovation Centre shows that the companies that embrace their stakeholders are the ones that perform best. Companies achieve success through a 'high-productivity' equilibrium of investing in skills and building strong relationships of trust with customers and the public, not through a 'low-productivity' equilibrium – today's conspicuous model – of squeezing the most out of the least investment with the highest margin and executive pay possible.

Exorbitant executive pay is the defining scandal of the Thatcherite economy, mushrooming beyond any semblance of true worth. At £4.5 million, the average remuneration of chief executives of Britain's top hundred companies in 2016 was 160 times that of their average employee. For every pound of company turnover, top pay is now as high, and sometimes higher, than in comparable US companies. Directors are incentivised to put their own pay and immediate share price before the long-term interests of the firm. There needs to be a new stakeholder settlement. Every company's remuneration committee should include employee representatives and publish an annual fair pay report detailing the organisation's pay policy and explaining why employees at the top and bottom are paid as they are.

Constitutions of enterprise

There is a corrosion, verging on collapse, of public trust in business ethics. The way to reverse it is for companies to embrace their stakeholders and commit themselves to social and public objectives as part of their commercial purpose in their constitutions. This is the cornerstone of stakeholder capitalism.

A celebrated model is the John Lewis Partnership. Equally exemplary is Welsh Water, the only mutually owned water utility, which has outperformed water utilities owned by profit-maximising PLCs or by private equity outfits. Likewise, the Building Society Association recently demonstrated that mutually owned building societies enjoy more trust than banks and PLCs.

Shareholder-owned companies, with a brief to maximise short-term profits irrespective of ethical concerns, are not remotely the only viable form of business organisation. Britain has a great dearth of employee-owned companies, mutuals, co-operatives, trusts, partnerships, state companies and other enterprises overtly committed to delivering public benefit. It has only one fledgling publicly owned bank to support investment. There are no sovereign or citizen wealth funds, and almost no substantive pools of capital whose focus is on the long term.

Successful companies around the world are those that pursue clearly defined social purposes. By honouring these purposes, binding on shareholders, directors and employees alike, they mobilise their potential and build trust, loyalty and success. Profit is not the be-all and end-all, but one outcome of a clear social purpose.

The few British companies that currently exemplify stakeholder capitalism outperform other enterprises on the yardsticks that really matter – fulfilment in work, innovation, their green credentials, their long-term returns. For them, purpose is the 'north star': strong values holding stakeholders together in good times and bad, allowing commitment to innovation and investment on the basis of long-run success. That is why great companies set such store by their mission statements, whether eBay and its purpose to create 'a global trading platform where practically anyone can trade practically anything', or IKEA and its aim to 'create a better everyday life for the many people'. John Lewis proclaims its purpose as 'the happiness of its members' – maybe the best mission statement since the opening words of the United States Constitution. Pearson declares its purpose as 'to help people all over the world make progress in their lives through learning', while Unilever aims 'to make sustainable living commonplace'. These are not flights of rhetoric but invocations of the human spirit to do the best for their society in the 'little platoons' that Edmund Burke rightly described as the basis of all free societies.

To create this new stakeholder capitalism, there needs to be a challenge to the prevailing institution of the public limited company (PLC) – which is public only in the restricted sense that its shares are quoted on public stock exchanges. Beyond that, PLCs have no avowed public mission and minimal duties. We propose that companies be required by law to declare their purposes in accessible constitutions, and to report regularly to their owners, the public and appropriate regulatory bodies on how they are fulfilling them. The limp provisions on 'corporate purpose' in the 2006 Companies Act need to be massively enhanced.

Companies need 'anchored' shareholders who embrace their vision, with new pools of capital from which such shareholders can be drawn. In Germany and Scandinavia companies typically have a few core, anchor shareholders – 'block-holders' – constituting a critical mass of the voting rights, who in effect control the company and give it long-term loyalty. The shareholder base of British companies is the most fragmented and selfish in the industrialised West.

Britain should use every tool in the policy locker – tax, regulation, law, creating new pools of capital – to foster more block-holders. It should be block-holders and other long-term shareholders who vote on companies' futures during take-overs. Only those shareholders on the register at the time any takeover is launched should vote – not the motley bunch of arbitrageurs and hedge-fund jackals who recently settled GKN's fate, having bought shares after the bid was announced only to make a quick profit by selling to the highest bidder regardless of the future of the company.

We need radically to create and expand alternative versions of ownership. In his 1926 essay against laissez-faire, Keynes argued that 'in many cases the ideal size for the unit of control and organisation lies somewhere between the individual and the modern State. I suggest, therefore, that progress lies in the growth and the recognition of semi-autonomous bodies within the State – bodies whose criterion of action within their own field is solely the public good as they understand it.' Keynes was appealing for the creation not of monolithic state-owned and directed companies on the model of Attlee's nationalisations of coal, steel and rail, but for something more plural: smaller, autonomous state-sponsored companies with constitutions committed to the public good, not high profits as their cardinal function. The East Coast public company that took over from a failing private operator of the London to Edinburgh rail line after 2009 is a good example.

Stakeholder capitalism requires a new generation of 'public benefit' companies tasked in their constitutions to take into account environmental, social or public objectives. A regulated utility or a social media provider could incorporate as this kind of company, declaring its purpose as, say, 'to deliver the best water possible at the cheapest price', or 'to inform, educate and entertain' (the founding mission of the BBC). In such companies, customers and employees should be represented on the board. Even in the hardest commercial context, retail for example, businesses especially dependent on the good will of employees and customers might wish to take this form.

The PLC model has lost public confidence almost entirely in the sphere of utilities and infrastructure, where profit targets and dividends have, since Thatcher's privatisations, consistently overridden the interests of citizens. Thames Water is an egregious example, accumulating sky-high debts and distributing vast dividends to its private equity owners via a tax-efficient vehicle in Luxembourg, who then sold out. BT's investment in high-speed broadband has been slow and inadequate, and few would argue that the first target of the rail operators has been good-value passenger service. The 2018 debacle of Stagecoach and Virgin, who four years earlier were controversially awarded the East Coast rail contract in place of the previous public company, being permitted to walk out early on £2 billion of contractual commitments to the taxpayer has done more for the cause of nationalisation than Jeremy Corbyn and Karl Marx put together.

Instead of spending at least £170 billion on renationalisation as the 2017 Labour manifesto implied, a stakeholder government could take a 'foundation' share in each privatised utility. This would require each utility to become a public benefit company (PBC), declaring its purpose as to promote the public good while seeking to make a reasonable surplus and no more. The foundation share would enable the government to appoint independent non-executive directors to help secure this purpose. These public benefit companies would be required to remain domiciled in the UK for tax purposes. They would report regularly, explaining how the public interest was being served.

PBCs on this model would combine the best of the public and private sectors. Nor should we stop there. Employee ownership in Britain is paltry. Mutually owned Employee Ownership Trusts (EOTs) could, with state encouragement, employ three million people within a decade. Co-operatives and mutuals could be multiplied to employ over a million if encouraged by a state development bank that supported them financially. There should be tax breaks for individuals establishing EOTs, mutuals and co-operatives. A constitutional template should be developed for a pure stakeholder company that builds the participation of consumers, employees and supply chains into its management and governance. The pure devil-take-the-hindmost, short-term share price-maximising firm should become a minority form.

Existing company owners and asset managers need to start taking 'intrinsic purpose' seriously. Britain's £7 trillion asset-management industry doesn't remotely do this at present. Long-term stewardship of companies is not a priority for most shareholders, asset managers, occupational pension funds and insurance companies who invest in British companies. In any case, many of the forty thousand pension funds are too small to act as company stewards, and with insurance companies only own 8.1 per cent of all British shares. Foreign ownership now amounts to 53.9 per cent of all British shares, and although some are signalling a welcome interest in supporting long-term value-generation, this is far from common.

To turn owners into stewards, asset-management companies of whatever nationality should be required to declare their purposes and report on their delivery. The Financial Reporting Council, whose role at present is essentially advisory, should be given real teeth.

New sources of finance are essential to stakeholder capital-ism. Local authority pension funds are being merged to create 'superfunds'. They should only give mandates to investment managers who subscribe to stakeholder objectives. Pools of sav-ings should be made to work for the good of both the saver and the wider economy. The fast-growing private pension funds that are now replacing unsustainable final-salary schemes are set to grow to over £500 billion by 2030. They should follow suit and the opportunity to boost ownership of British companies be grasped. This could create a pool of £100 billion of equity capital for purposeful companies.

A Citizens' Wealth Fund should be created from receipts

from the sale of public assets as well as from revenues from
a tax on dividends (a 'scrip tax'). Like the sovereign wealth
funds of Norway and Singapore, this fund would be managed
in Keynesian style by an independent board as an autonomous
organisation on behalf of the public. One objective would be to
become a block-holder in purposeful companies. A new National
Infrastructure Bank should also be created to provide long-term
loans for the transformation of Britain's creaking infrastructure.

Digital goliaths

Facebook and Google are flagships of a fleet of high-tech data
monopolists. Big is good in the digital universe. Even bigger
is better still. Analogue capitalism is also consolidating and
merging into ever-bigger entities.

The growing concentration of corporate power is awesome.
In every industry the market power and profits of the biggest
companies have been surging into a new 'virulent capitalism'
unconstrained by checks and balances and still less by national
boundaries. Hence the share of profits in national income has
risen while the share going to labour has fallen consistently
since the 1970s and is now close to an all-time low.

It used to be an economic law that as companies got larger
they became more inefficient, which was a check on monopoly. But in today's digital marketplace, the more is 'produced',
the cheaper every successive unit becomes, pretty much
indefinitely. A key attraction of Facebook, Spotify, Uber,
Amazon and Airbnb is their very size. Far from their managers losing control, Artificial Intelligence and computerised

techniques allow costs – from wages to how production lines, supply chains and warehouses are organised – to be ever more efficiently managed as they expand. Meanwhile, for users, the bigger the network and search engine, the more efficient. Google is the search engine of choice because of its scale. Facebook has done the same for social media. Uber is now a national and international smartphone cab service. Airbnb has become the means to find a room anywhere in the world. We use and value them because of the ubiquity and user-friendliness of their digital systems, scale breeding scale.

Monopoly corrupts and exploits, and the public soon pays dearly. Amazon secures extortionate discounts from its suppliers, who recoup what they have lost by raising the prices they charge to other retailers, who are going to the wall. Uber is burning through investors' cash to subsidise cheap rides, waiting for the day it will wipe out enough of its competitors to raise prices and supress the 'receipts' of the cynically named 'partners' who are in reality drivers employed with practically no employment rights. Facebook is siphoning advertising that previously supported journalism and other content provision. Google and Facebook alone account for half of all digital advertising revenue.

What the goliaths can't achieve by market force they achieve by takeover, buying out competitors present and future – the 'kill in the crib' strategy. Facebook has bought WhatsApp, Microsoft owns LinkedIn and Google YouTube, along with over two hundred small companies that might have become challengers but are now poodles.

As these digital goliaths achieve unassailable market power, aspiring entrepreneurs without immense courage and funding tend to flee, another law of monopoly playing out in the tech universe. In the US young firms have been declining as a share of the economy for forty years; so too in Britain. Yet without the challenge of new entrants, incumbents have fewer incentives to improve old products or create new ones, which may be one reason why business investment has stagnated over the past fifteen years.

The regulators' thresholds for considering whether an acquisition will entrench a buyer's predatory market power are far too low. Google's Eric Schmidt bluntly boasts about this. 'The company made the decision,' he said in 2011, 'to accelerate our rate of acquisition of small companies. Because it is the fastest way to fill out some of [our] broader strategies.' These companies were below the anti-trust threshold, and not subject to Federal Trade Commission notification or waiting periods.

Britain needs to get wiser about these new market dynamics. The Competition and Markets Authority needs urgently to curb the digital goliaths, by encouraging not suppressing competitors. We also require a new rights-based approach to personal data. Used properly, data – the new 'oil' propelling the digital revolution – has the potential to create enormous public good, including a generation of new companies. Under a data charter (proposed by the Big Innovation Centre) not only individuals should be given an opt-in power over the use of their data; there should be simple rights of redress against misuse and codes of ethics. The aim should be to create clarity over data ownership and use, as part of the new social contract, and in so doing create forces that countervail the market dynamics feeding monopoly. We need to hold high-tech companies to ever-higher standards of transparency and accountability. Where private digital platforms like Google have unassailable monopoly power, they should be required to become public benefit companies.

However, Britain needs to face the reality that action on a national scale is palpably inadequate to confront the goliaths. There is only one effective countervailing force at work: the European Union. The challenge is simple: to insist that the companies are socially responsible. Only the EU has success-fully challenged Google's monopoly, fining the company 2.4 billion euros for favouring its own Google shopping comparison sites, and making Facebook and Amazon pay more tax. The EU is now considering breaking up Google. No single European state could hope to achieve this alone.

The vast harvesting of personal data by the goliaths is espe-cially dangerous, as in the scandal over Cambridge Analytica's use of Facebook data to develop an online tool that may have influenced elections and the Brexit referendum. Here again it is the EU's General Data Protection Regulation, introduced as we write, that offers effective public protection. Only at EU level can consumers and citizens resist the goliaths on anything from tax to data without, in all likelihood, losing their services or being forced to retreat. The same is true of the non-digital goliaths over, say, diesel emissions or plastic packaging.

International trade is not a football league of equally matched teams waiting with open arms for a newly promoted Britain, energised by leaving the EU, to join up and score hat-tricks. It is a dog-eat-dog world in which the choice for a medium-sized country is either to make common cause with one of the three economic blocs – namely China, the US or the EU – capable of challenging the new monopolists and cartels, or to roll over undefended and be plundered.

New Model Unions

In the two centuries since the Industrial Revolution, and the 150 years since the legalisation of trade unions, the power of workers to stand up to monopolist employers in order to secure decent wages and working conditions has rarely been weaker.

Unions are now largely restricted to the public sector, where their public image is often poor, in part because of strikes. Across the private sector, trade unions have been eviscerated. Less than 15 per cent of the UK's private-sector workforce of 25 million are now members of trade unions, a staggering reduction of two-thirds from 45 per cent in 1979. Anti-union laws, the cultural stigmatisation of 'organised labour', and the difficulty anyway of organising in multiple small workplaces, have taken their toll. The decline is starkest in the hospitality sector – bars, restaurants and hotels – where union membership is just 2.5 per cent.

Because there are few strong private-sector unions, the share of national income accruing to wages is falling, working conditions are growing more insecure, and common bonds between workers and managers are tenuous. In today's virulent capitalism, there is little capacity to challenge the new goliaths of the workplace and the scope for abusive behaviour widens.

Unions need reinventing as social partners and co-creators of stakeholder capitalism. They need to be more like guilds, guarantors of skills and fair wages, than confrontational representatives of a shrinking working class. While fighting zero-hours contracts and workplace insecurity, 'new model unions' should also strike out anew, creating employee mutuals run on good work principles.

'New model unions' should champion companies that pioneer profit sharing, and employee share ownership and trusts. As shareholders in pension funds they should promote stakeholder values. They should promote and provide apprenticeships, and help transform skill levels for young and older workers alike. They should open the way to good pension advice, put forward skilled pension fund trustees to represent workforces, skilled remuneration directors to sit on company remuneration committees and rein in executive pay, and qualified non-executive directors for company boards. They should aim, as in Germany, to play an active part in holding company chiefs to account for the delivery of their purpose; partners not enemies of enterprise.

To boost membership, new model unions should imitate the AA, offering instant breakdown cover to non-members. Workers could be sold services in exchange for a fee, rather than having to be a member before problems arise. There should be a single joining form to become a union member, with discounts for younger workers and apps for workplaces where it is hard to organise. More than a million private-sector workers could soon be recruited by these means, estimates the Fabian Society.

Successful unions legitimise employers and generate trust on thorny issues like executive pay. They convince management to negotiate company-wide wage deals and consult on major

changes like takeovers, relocations, redundancy and hiring programmes, to secure employee buy-in and higher productivity.
There are bound to be tensions, sometimes conflict, but good
faith collective bargaining, with transparency on both sides and
an acceptance that deals must stick, helps build stakeholder
capitalism.

If all this seems a pipedream, consider the path-breaking
2014 Social Covenant signed by EDF Energy and four unions –
GMB, Prospect, UCATT and Unite – to create a framework for
'just pay, industrial relations, recruitment, health and welfare,
skills development and workforce communications' for the
multi-billion nuclear construction site at Hinkley Point C in
Somerset. BT, likewise, has invested millions in developing the
leadership skills of union frontline and middle-level leaders, to
foster an *esprit de corps* and a shared mission. This is new model
unionism in action.

The new social contract

After announcing that 'there is no such thing as society',
Margaret Thatcher went on: 'there are individual men and
women and there are families'.

Thatcher obviously did not intend there to be no state at all,
just no welfare state of the kind advanced by Attlee, Bevan and
Beveridge. She preached a sermon to the General Assembly of
the Church of Scotland on the text: 'If a man will not work he
shall not eat.' Her moral imperative, which animates her Brexit
disciples, was for individuals not to be 'cocooned' by a state
that 'squanders' the earnings and wealth of individuals. The

entire moral fibre of the nation was at risk from 'state social-ism'. Tellingly, when David Cameron felt impelled to distance himself from his predecessor on 'society', he did so while subtly denying its democratic expression: 'There is such a thing as society, it's just not the same thing as the state.'

The truth is that in any civilisation there is such a thing as society, and the state's role is to underpin and defend it. There is far more to a healthy society than the state, but public action is vital for strengthening reciprocal bonds between indi-viduals, institutions and the community. There is no strong society without a strong and accountable state based on a strong social contract.

Britain has a weak implicit social contract; it needs a strong, explicit one. After decades where Conservative social policy has largely been 'austerity for the poor and welfare for the rich', public services are squeezed and in many areas, especially in social care, threadbare. Unemployment benefit and social security have been serially diminished in opaque and euphemis-tically titled but invariably cost-reducing reforms. The NHS and education are pitched from one crisis to the next with funding determined by minimum electoral – not citizen – requirements.

So many of the ills besetting Britain have their origins in the refusal to forge a decent social contract. The housing and social mobility crises, the re-emergence of desperate poverty and the lack of skills of so many young people – all flow from this.

Not all Tories, even on the right, accept raw Thatcherism. But with the withering of the One Nation tradition, too many settle for the neo-liberal assertion that anything beyond 'safety-net' welfare and middling public services are essentially impractical and unaffordable, however desirable. When the word 'Scandinavia' is mentioned as a counter – as in the 2010 book *The Spirit Level: Why Equality is Better for Everyone*, by Richard Wilkinson and Kate Pickett, and the 2014 international bestseller *Capital in the Twenty-First Century* by French economist Thomas Piketty – it is met with the self-serving riposte that Scandinavian-style taxation of the better-off would be 'impossible' in free-market Britain, although it works in Denmark, Finland, Norway and Sweden. One Nation Tories believing the contrary have become a dwindling rump.

The result is Brexit Britain, where the disadvantaged bear the brunt of austerity while mainstream public services are at best so-so and at worst pitiful. The better-off, meanwhile, insulate themselves where they can with private health and education and financially – if not physically – gated communities.

Virtually all the burden of the post-2010 fiscal adjustment has been borne by public spending cuts. Spending on public services per head will have fallen by nearly a quarter between 2010 and 2020, with the baleful outcomes described in chapter 1. The NHS budget, which increased at 8.6 per cent a year in real terms between 2001–2 and 2004–5, will have increased just 1.1 per cent a year between 2009–10 and 2020–1. The NHS is now needing emergency relief to head off a national health crisis.

The NHS has among the lowest per-capita numbers of doctors, nurses and hospital beds in the Western world, the third-lowest number of doctors and hospital beds per head of twenty-one developed nations, and the sixth-lowest number of nurses. Yet by international standards the NHS is highly efficient, producing good health outcomes for much less than comparable countries spend. But under Conservative governments there is an entrenched refusal to fund it properly, culminating in unparalleled pressure during the winter of 2017/18. Poignantly, the post-2010 Health Secretary, Andrew Lansley, confessed that his colon cancer was not identified early by the NHS because of funding cuts.

Some of the most serious cuts of all, bordering on the obscene, are in prisons and criminal justice. Churchill, when Home Secretary, remarked that the civilisation of a society can be judged by its prisons. Britain's prisons are hellholes that disgrace us all. The prison population has trebled in forty years, yet since 2010 spending has been slashed by a third. Suicides (119 in 2016 alone) and violence have soared; rehabilitation and decency have collapsed. Funding for the entire infrastructure of criminal justice – not just prisons but also policing, probation, legal aid, victim support – has been brutally cut. Decency must be restored. We should tackle the prison crisis by following President Macron's policy in France of turning short sentences for non-violent crimes into tough community sentences with prison only for those who do not obey.

With a 40 per cent fall in local government spending since 2010, many authorities can barely meet their minimum statutory obligations. From flood defences to school class sizes, police numbers, under-fives services and social care for the elderly, local services are in ruins. Investment in public infrastructure has been neglected, the World Economic Forum recently ranking the quality of Britain's infrastructure twenty-seventh in the world, down from nineteenth in 2006.

The National Infrastructure Commission has identified a

dozen vital projects palsied by the stop–go approach to investment – the third runway at Heathrow, High Speed 2 and 3 (linking the major northern cities from Liverpool to Newcastle and Hull), Crossrail 2 (linking north-east, central and south-west London), eastern crossings of the River Thames, flexible power systems, renewable and decarbonised energy, Hinkley Point C, broadband and mobile, 5G mobile and the water and flood-defence infrastructure. Apart from HS2, most of these are not happening or, in the case of energy and digital, and Crossrail 2 and HS3, only stumbling along.

In his 2018 budget Chancellor Philip Hammond signalled that with day-to-day public spending now being matched by day-to-day receipts, austerity might be fractionally eased. Yet public spending is still projected to decline as a proportion of GDP, with ongoing real-terms cuts. The new bogeyman for which all this privation is being justified is no longer the annual public sector deficit – it is the national debt. Only an increase in taxes of more than £40 billion, estimates the Institute for Fiscal Studies, can allow Hammond's self-imposed debt and deficit targets to be met, while public spending is maintained in real terms.

The obsession with cutting national debt even while the economy is weak has no grounding in successful Keynesian economics. National debt has been proportionally far higher than today for most of the last three hundred years, because of frequent wars. It is not austerity, but the avoidance of war and unnecessarily deep recessions, that is critical to reducing national debt over time.

Moreover, Britain is fortunate: thanks to successful

long-termism on the part of the Bank of England, its public debt is held in long-term bonds redeemable on average over fourteen years, and a high proportion is held by British savings and investment institutions, reducing the country's vulnerability to a sell-off from panicky international investors. With interest rates at a near three-hundred-year low, the country emphatically does not have a public debt crisis. There is no need for austerity. The social contract does not have to become a human sacrifice on the altar of austerity and debt reduction.

Nor are fair taxes on the wealthy and corporations harmful. The IMF finds no evidence that properly designed higher rates of income and inheritance tax on the better-off result in lower growth rates. Nor is there evidence that lowering already-low corporation tax materially boosts investment and growth: companies invest for pre-tax rather than post-tax returns, and if those expected returns are not high, they use cash from corporation tax cuts to buy back shares, take over smaller companies to build a stronger position, or simply hoard cash rather than invest. The neoliberal argument is essentially a plea to enrich the rich, not an argument for efficiency, let alone justice.

There is finance within reach for Britain to fund a decent social contract: it just needs the courage and will to raise it.

The starting point should be fair taxation of property. House prices are at an all-time high in relation to income, housing equity tops £6 trillion, and London property has, in effect, become the largest onshore tax haven in the world. Yet residential property values have absurdly not been revalued for local tax purposes since 1991, and no less incredibly property valued over £320,000 pays no additional tax whatever because of the distorted system of 'bands and caps' introduced in 1991 to slash taxes on the better-off. The virtual exemption from tax of higher-value property is a huge welfare handout to the better-off, especially the very rich; it is also a principal driver of austerity for the poor, since local social services are financed by this property tax. The existing banded council tax should be replaced by a straightforward percentage tax on current property values. All the income should go to fund better local services.

Property tax evasion also needs to be outlawed. Every property owner should be required to register their identity rather than hiding behind anonymous offshore companies, shell within shell, Russian-doll style. Years ago the government promised such a property register; nothing happened. The *Financial Times* estimates the total value of the assets of unidentified property owners to exceed £100 billion, and their anonymity is designed largely to evade tax. Those who fail to pay tax should lose their property.

It is also wrong, and a severe limitation of community resources, that so little of the gain from property development goes to local and national government. Development gains should not be pocketed largely by property developers. Attlee's post-war government nationalised development gains from major land transactions, a policy dismantled by its Tory successors. There should be a land value tax on the market value of land as it rises, so as to capture unearned windfalls. Government also needs stronger compulsory purchase powers to buy land at existing use value, so that any rise in values can be redeployed for reinvestment in infrastructure and services.

These powers should be put into action to create a new generation of new towns and cities and to replace social housing sold off over the last forty years. England's last major new town, Milton Keynes, was founded fifty years ago, and the absence of any successors is part of the reason for sky-high property values and the raging housing crisis in London and southern England.

Inheritance tax has become a voluntary tax. Only £5 billion is raised from inheritance tax, less than 0.1 per cent of the value of Britain's housing stock alone, excluding businesses and land. This is why wealth inequality in even greater than income inequality in modern Britain. The aim should be to at least double the yield. The right say 'death taxes' deters enterprise, because the chief impulse of any entrepreneur is to pass his or her wealth on to their children – which is palpable nonsense. The impulse to succeed in life is not to ensure that your children never have to work. In any case, entrepreneurs do not pay the tax; their children do, who have done nothing to earn their inheritance except to turn up in the right maternity ward. Almost every modern democratic society taxes inheritance substantially; only today's Thatcherites have the brass neck to argue that wealth should be dynastic, with no obligation to the wider community in which the lucky inheritors live, and which gives them a society worth living in.

There are many other fair taxes. VAT could be extended to financial services; environmental harm, like the use of plastics and disposable coffee cups, could be taxed; the highest rate of income tax on those earning over £150,000 a year, cut below 50 per cent by George Osborne, should be raised.

Together, these sources of fair taxation would yield tens of billions a year, which should be used to cut taxes on the poor and fund a new social contract in health, education, housing, immigration, social care for the elderly, under-fives centres and other local services. Homelessness, a blight on a rich and civilised society, should be consigned to history with a national system of hostels for rough sleepers. There should be a big new Immigrant Impact Fund investing in localities with larger numbers of immigrants, so that the pressure on local services is met and the 'national' benefits of immigration, in terms of extra tax revenue from people who mainly work extremely hard, are shared with the communities where they reside and which their labours serve. The NHS could offer a universal dental service, and stop the scandal of people having to buy £10 DIY dental care kits.

The new Citizens' Wealth Fund, together with local government bonds, should fund a revolution in infrastructure and public housing. All the priority projects identified by the National Infrastructure Commission should be launched, starting with universal broadband and 4G mobile coverage, and a new 'Crossrail of the North' to transform connectivity between the northern cities of England. So much needs to be done to give people a decent chance in life, to support the disadvantaged, to help integrate immigrants, to regenerate local communities, to solve the housing crisis. With a will, stakeholder capitalism and a new social contract can achieve this, creating a decent economy and society in which the mass of our citizens can flourish.

Food banks and homelessness symbolise more than anything else the dilapidated state of our society. One stakeholder reform could significantly help those who suffer these extremes: a legal obligation on all food retailers to give their unsold food to food banks, homeless shelters, churches and other social enterprises. Food is not just about profit, it is about decency – and survival.

Honouring our young

The neglect of Britain's young is the most acute and shameful consequence of our disintegrating social contract.

The English education system is essentially geared to produce about a hundred thousand eighteen-year-olds who each year go to the top twenty-four Russell Group universities, a disproportionate number of whom are educated privately. These are the privileged few for whom the education system is robust and delivers solid outcomes – although with Brexit casting a pall over our economy, even for them less good than in the past.

There is a yawning gulf between the privileges afforded by this system of elite schools and universities, leading to the predominantly London-based professions, and the chaotic, unsystematic approach to supporting the half a million or so teenagers each year who do not go to university. A revolution in education and skills is a foundation pillar of stakeholder capitalism, from tackling social and regional inequalities to building strong companies and decent incomes and conditions for their employees.

In much of the country, especially the social mobility coldspots described in chapter 1, the education system is inadequate, with underpaid and overstretched teachers in poor facilities simply unable to compensate for home backgrounds and lack of aspirations. As their students emerge from the classroom and want, say, to become a plumber, they confront thirty-three qualifications offered at three different levels by five different awarding organisations. Neither the aspirant plumber nor the companies for which she and he might work have a clear idea of the value of whatever qualification they gain, though the chances are, notoriously, that the course will have been cheap, not very demanding and the qualification not worth much.

The consequences can be seen nation-wide in the poor skills of young people, and the difficulty for those without good degrees in getting jobs with decent pay and prospects. Over the past thirty years, the skills policy that has delivered this debacle has been overseen by sixty-five secretaries of state in eleven different departments in a tragic game of human pass-the-parcel.

As long ago as 1884 a royal commission on technical education reported: 'The one point in which Germany is overwhelmingly superior to England is in schools ... the dense ignorance so common among workmen in England is unknown in Germany.' Nearly a century and a half later, England provides decent apprenticeships for less than half the proportion of school-leavers supported in Germany, Denmark, the Netherlands and Norway (20 per cent, as against 40/50 per cent). British employers are quick to spot that EU ex-trainees are willing to work for lower wages and are often better skilled and motivated than their young British counterparts.

To appear to be doing something about this apprenticeship drought, David Cameron introduced an apprenticeship levy on employers in 2016. With great fanfare before the 2015 election, he plucked from the air a target of three million new apprenticeships between 2015 and 2020, to be funded by this levy.

But there has been so little state leadership and so much state inertia that the number of apprentices has actually fallen by a third since the start of the levy. Worse, the 'skills' system is overlaid on a myriad of craft qualifications, competing and often low-grade providers and certification bodies, and little financial support for young people, especially from disadvantaged backgrounds, while they train.

There should be a wholly new publicly led approach. Every eighteen-year-old not going to university should be guaranteed an apprenticeship place, with the state acting as provider of last resort where insufficient apprenticeships are on offer from private- and public-sector employers. The delivery of apprenticeships and further education ought to be prime responsibilities for local government and mayors, with funding and responsibility devolved. The government should require every large public service organisation, including the civil service, the NHS and local authorities, to recruit at least as many apprentices as graduates in the ranks of their young trainees. Across the public and private sectors, the apprenticeship levy should be tied contractually to a significant increase in the number and quality of apprenticeships year by year.

There is no apprenticeship equivalent of the UCAS system that for decades has enabled academic teenagers to choose and access university courses as a rite of passage. The state does nothing to create or support a proper clearing system for school-leavers not going on to university. Nor does it offer funding for these young people – a large majority of each cohort – at a rate remotely comparable to that offered to the minority who gain decent A-level grades and a university offer through

UCAS. There should be a single lifelong tertiary educational entitlement available to every person. Apprenticeship is the Cinderella of England's education and training system: it should be the princess.

The one unambiguously successful initiative in technical education since the war was the national system of colleges of advanced technology and polytechnics set up in the 1960s, which equipped a generation of young people with good technical diplomas and degrees. They were institutions with powerful city and regional missions, engaging directly with employers. These colleges and polytechnics were converted into conventional universities in the 1990s. To meet the imperative for more higher-level technical education to degree level, the best of today's further education colleges should form a new generation of polytechnics, in partnership with employers in the public and private sectors. At least ten of these new advanced polytechnics, one or more for each region of England, should be established with urgency.

The voice of the neglected young is virtually non-existent in the national debate, which is partly why things are so bad. Teenagers don't get the vote until they are eighteen; even then most of them, particularly from low-income families, don't use it. There is barely any citizenship education in schools; even the system for registering eighteen-/nineteen-year-olds to vote is hit-and-miss. All of this needs to change radically, including a lowering of the voting age to sixteen, as we propose in the next chapter.

Neglect starts at birth. In 2016, a third of five-year-olds began school without a proper level of 'development', defined as being able to listen to, understand and follow instructions, use the past, present and future tenses correctly, read and understand simple sentences, talk about their feelings, and count and carry out simple addition and subtraction. Among low-income families, the third rose to nearly half; and the geographical divergence is equally stark. Twice as many children start school without this basic standard of development in Middlesbrough in the north-east compared with Greenwich in London, despite the many council estates and poor communities in that part of south-east London.

The cities and regions of left-behind Britain need an Education Marshall Plan. After decades of governments urging private schools to behave like the charities they legally are, but seeing virtually nothing happen, we should tax private school fees. An educational opportunity tax of 25 per cent on private school fees would raise around £2.5 billion towards this Marshall Plan. It could be used to boost teacher pay in hard-to-recruit areas; fund one-to-one or small-group tuition for children in danger of not getting English and maths GCSEs, the indispensable passports to skilled work and further learning; and fund free music and sports tuition – provided partly in and by private schools, which have excellent facilities in these areas, for which they would be paid from part of the proceeds of the new tax. All children should enjoy the wider opportunities that private school pupils take for granted. Doing it this way, alongside the wholesale expansion of National Citizen Service, also proposed in the next chapter, would help to bridge the private–state school divide and eliminate the ignorance that too many young people have of any part of the country besides their own.

We must also tackle the scourge of school expulsions, which cause so many young lives to go completely off the rails. A distressingly high proportion of children excluded from school before the age of sixteen, abandoned by society, end up in prison within a few years. Schools should be forbidden from expelling pupils except in extreme cases and there should be no temporary exclusions. Instead, schools should be required and funded to make appropriate on-site provision for disruptive pupils, even if, for good reasons, they cannot always be taught in mainstream classrooms.

Part of the income from extra taxes on the better-off should go to cut university tuition fees. Most students go on to better-paid jobs and come from better-off families, so this would essentially be a fair redistribution between generations. Since the trebling of tuition fees to £9000 a year in 2010 (now £9250), students in England pay the highest average university fees in the world, although most of them will not fully repay the debts they incur, displacing the cost onto the next generation of taxpayers. A fair system would see fees substantially and immediately reduced to a level of sustainable repayment, with the balance supplemented by today's tax revenues. Vice-chancellors should give a hand by cutting their mega pay of up to £500,000.

In all these ways, it is time to build a new stakeholder capitalism and a new social contract, reducing poverty, boosting prosperity, and creating genuine opportunity for all young people. Too much of Britain is too poor, too divided, too unproductive, too alienated. It needs to be enfranchised – by a stronger economy and society, and by a better political system, as we now set out to describe.

6

Taking back real control

Shortly before the Brexit referendum, the Queen led celebrations commemorating the eight-hundredth anniversary of Magna Carta, and of the medieval oppressed 'taking back control' from their oppressors.

Celebrating a medieval royal charter exposes, more than anything, the absence of a constitution of liberty and equality in modern Britain. It is time for a contemporary Great Charter to give real control to the nations, cities and localities of Britain – particularly in overcentralised England, a nation of 53 million people, more than five times the population of Scotland, Wales and Northern Ireland combined. England is run from Whitehall like a virtual colony. The Great Charter should proclaim the end of democratic feudalism. Radical devolution should revitalise England's cities and counties, giving them the duty to regenerate England and tackle in our age Beveridge's five giants of Want, Disease, Ignorance, Squalor and Idleness.

A central argument of this book is that Brexit's core aim is to achieve 'Thatcherism in one country', essentially on behalf of the rich and successful of London and the southern Home Counties. The Brexit-Thatcherites dress up their ambitions in the language of sovereignty, 'taking back control', and breaking free from the regulatory incubus of 'Brussels', but their intention is a ruthless power grab, executed by control of the Conservative Party and ruling through an untrammelled House of Commons, where in seven of the ten elections since coming to power in 1979 the Tories have been the largest party.

The well-oiled mechanisms of Thatcherism in one country are 'control or abolish' and 'winner takes all' within the Westminster system. Hence the effective demolition of independent city and local government. Hence too Brexit, which seeks to abolish the European tier of government and legitimacy which has constrained the Thatcherites. Only devolution to Scotland, Wales, Northern Ireland and London has mitigated the constitutional march of Thatcherism since 1979, but this affects only a small proportion of the UK population. Most of England has no devolution worth the name.

In order to 'take back real control' individual measures of devolution are not enough. Devolution needs to be entrenched in Parliament itself. The Great Charter should replace the House of Lords with a Federal Senate of the United Kingdom, with a mission to defend devolution and the interests of local communities across the UK. The Great Charter would also declare the social rights and responsibilities of the British people.

Brexit's proponents claim that it promises a new power settlement for the UK. The problem is that it is the wrong one: power needs to flow down from Westminster, not be funnelled still further into a hegemonic House of Commons and Whitehall, which govern so badly.

A civilisation of liberty

The dazzling poet and novelist Ben Okri says that a nation's written constitution is 'the best story a people can tell about itself to itself'. For all its traditions of liberty, Britain has no written constitution that tells the story of the rights, values, duties, ambitions and institutions of the British people. This leads Okri to describe Brexit as 'a failure of citizenship'.

The Conservative conceit is that a written constitution is not necessary because liberty is uniquely inscribed in British DNA, protected by Parliament and the common law. The truth is the existing settlement has become a mechanism for injustice, extreme partisanship and overcentralisation, breeding an impoverished view of citizenship and the public interest. One of the central principles of Enlightenment thinking is the creation of a citizenry who uphold a public sphere of which government and Parliament, constrained by a written constitution, are but part. No such tradition is embodied in Britain's constitution, as evidenced by our patchwork of inequality of opportunity, quiet suffering and enfeebled local communities.

The only written constitution of which Britain is a part is Europe's. And what a constitution it is! Here is the preamble of the Treaty of Paris of 1951 – the Magna Carta of Modern Europe – which in effect established the European Union:

THE PRESIDENT OF THE FEDERAL REPUBLIC OF GERMANY, THE PRINCE ROYAL OF BELGIUM, THE PRESIDENT OF THE FRENCH REPUBLIC, THE PRESIDENT OF THE ITALIAN REPUBLIC, THE GRAND DUCHESS OF LUXEMBOURG, THE QUEEN OF THE NETHERLANDS,

CONSIDERING that world peace can be safeguarded only by creative efforts commensurate with the dangers that threaten it,

CONVINCED that the contribution which an organised and vital Europe can make to civilisation is indispensable to the maintenance of peaceful relations,

RECOGNISING that Europe can be built only through practical achievements which will first of all create real solidarity, and through the establishment of common bases for economic development,

RESOLVED to substitute for age-old rivalries the merging of their essential interests; to create, by establishing an economic community, the basis for a broader and deeper community among peoples long divided by bloody conflicts; and to lay the foundations for institutions which will give direction to a destiny henceforward shared,

HAVE DECIDED to create a European Coal and Steel Community.

Eight centuries after Magna Carta, rather than seeking to destroy the constitution of Europe, it is time for the Queen and Parliament to proclaim a British constitution as good as this. The Great Charter of Modern Britain should open thus:

ELIZABETH THE SECOND by the Grace of God of the United Kingdom of Great Britain and Northern Ireland Queen,

PROUD of the United Kingdom as a civilisation of liberty and an inspiration to the world,

RECOGNISING that poverty, isolation and inequality disgrace our civilisation;

RESOLVED to disperse power to cities, counties and local communities across England, the largest of my kingdoms, from a Government in Westminster too remote and indifferent to their well-being,

CONSIDERING my bounden duty to promote peace and harmony throughout the island of Ireland, and to preserve devolution to Scotland, Wales and Northern Ireland,

CONVINCED that the United Kingdom is a vital part of the civilisation of Europe,

PROCLAIM THAT PARLIAMENT, pursuant to this Charter, will inaugurate a Federal Constitution of Liberty for the United Kingdom, which shall include a Statute of Local Self-Government for England, a Declaration of the Rights and Responsibilities of British citizens, a Federal Senate to assemble in the North of England, an extension of the vote to sixteen- and seventeen-year-old citizens, and a Declaration of Full Engagement in the European Union for the flourishing of the peoples of Europe.

It may not be on the level of Magna Carta's declarations forced by the barons from King John – 'To no one will we sell, to no one will we deny or delay right or justice . . . no free man is to be arrested, or imprisoned, or deprived of property, or in any way destroyed, save by the lawful judgement of his peers.' But it tries, within the same tradition, to civilise the relationships between governors and the governed and improve the quality of government.

The barons fighting for justice today are the millions in left-behind Britain who have little confidence in public institutions and virtually no belief that they work – or even aim to work – on their behalf. The new Great Charter needs to make citizens of modern Britain as proud of their institutions as the barons at Runnymede were of 'the common council of our kingdom'. It should be issued on 29 March 2019, the day when the authors of Brexit want to abandon Europe and annex to themselves a large part of the practical sovereignty of the British people.

In the Europe of 1215, Magna Carta was neither advanced nor unusual. It matters mainly for what it *started*. In the centuries after, England demonstrated a genius for representative and limited government, perhaps our greatest contribution to the human condition. Subsequent generations of English patriots – from Wat Tyler and the Peasants' Revolt to the Levellers, the Chartists and the Suffragettes – never ceased trying to 'take back real control'.

The historian Jeremy Catto explains:

Magna Carta is one of a European family of broadly similar medieval charters which articulate an emerging body of moral and cultural values. These values distinguish European civilisation, as it evolved in the second millennium, from the contemporary civilisations of Islam and China, and from the earlier Roman Empire. The King of England was matched by the King of Sicily, the Count of Flanders, the German Emperor.

Thanks in part to Britain's power and prestige, democratic institutions were introduced across Western Europe after the Second World War, and across Central and Eastern Europe after the fall of the Berlin Wall. The European Union is one of them, with its Parliament, Court, Council, Commission and Charter of Fundamental Rights. Yet only the complacent, ignoring the hard facts of history, could regard democracy across Europe as irreversible.

Twenty years ago, civil war and genocide overwhelmed Yugoslavia, an ancient territory of Europe. Dubrovnik, Srebrenica and Sarajevo rival the most unspeakable atrocities in history. They took place in our lifetime, forty years after the European Convention on Human Rights. An International Criminal Tribunal for Yugoslavia sat in The Hague from 1993, on the model of the Nuremberg trials. It concluded its trials only in 2017. It gave rise to the International Criminal Court, which has since attempted, feebly, to hold murderous dictators to account worldwide, following the example of Europe.

Democracy is fragile even in the core of the European Union. It took Germany five months to form a government after its 2017 election, in which the far right AfD party, including overt racists and neo-Nazis, polled 13 per cent and became the official opposition. Italy's 2018 election saw populist parties, led by the Five Star Movement and Lega Nord, win more than half the vote on an anti-immigrant tide. In 2016 Austria narrowly avoided electing its first far-right president, while in the 2017 French presidential election the Front National leader Marine Le Pen, lauding Nigel Farage and calling for 'Frexit', was runner-up. Spain is riven by the attempt of Catalonian nationalists to create a breakaway state. Further east, Poland and Hungary have authoritarian nativist governments in the shadow of Putin's Russia, an increasingly violent kleptocracy with fascist undercurrents. Hungary's Prime Minister Viktor Orbán boasts of transforming his country into an illiberal state. And practically all these populists and extremists get the thumbs up from US President Donald Trump. 'Is democracy dying?' was the cover article of the international journal *Foreign Affairs* in spring 2018.

Brexiters' facile answer is that these are reactions to the unaccountability and irresponsibility of the EU. Really? Too many other countries outside Europe are succumbing to the same anti-democratic trends for that to make any sense. The new reality is extreme partisan polarisation, affecting advanced democracies like the US as much as developing countries, by way of the Philippines and Turkey, which allows a 'strong man' to use the democratic process to come to power but then to sideline and subvert democratic institutions – the courts, the media, the opposition. Globalisation, disrupting economies and provoking mass migration of peoples, is generating a counter-reaction exploited by nationalist populists everywhere. Far from being the source of that counter-reaction, the EU is a bulwark against it.

So any notion that democracy in Europe is 'done' and that

we can now 'move on' is dangerously – perhaps even sui-cidally – complacent. It is a fallacy at the heart of Brexit. It is untrue even of the UK itself. At the time of writing, Northern Ireland is in its sixteenth month without a power-sharing administration because of the refusal of the political parties in the province to form one. Northern Ireland's nationalist com-munity, whose alienation and mistreatment underlay decades of 'troubles' and thousands of terrorist murders, is entirely unrepresented at Westminster.

To live on as a beacon of freedom and civilisation, Britain needs to make power-sharing work in Northern Ireland and extend devolution successfully to England. And Britain must stay deeply engaged with Europe's other democracies and the European Union: to strengthen them is to strengthen itself. Solidarity between Europe's democracies is equally indispen-sable to projecting European values, not least in Russia and China. To pursue 'England Alone' is as great a threat to the freedom as it is to the prosperity of both Britain and Europe.

No more 'control or abolish' and 'winner takes all'

The crisis in 'falling-to-pieces' Britain described in chapter 1 revolves around deep and growing inequality; it is also about geography. Swathes of England, remote in distance and atten-tion from London, are chronically poor, disempowered and embittered.

In Scotland and Wales, for all their continuing difficul-ties, devolution since 1999 has restored power and dignity to nations previously ruled by viceroys from imperial London.

The same now needs to happen, urgently, within England.

Ever since Henry VIII and his ruthless minister Thomas Cromwell, England has had a government subject only to intermittent parliamentary consent. Parliament is now democratically elected, but once it vests power in ministers, the government they form is an 'elected dictatorship', in the words of former Tory Lord Chancellor Lord Hailsham.

In some periods, local government in England has been given a meaningful role by Parliament. The Victorian era of Joseph Chamberlain and the 'civic fathers' was the high point of this quasi-devolution; indeed, during the nineteenth century more money was raised locally than nationally. But elected local government played a diminishing role in the postwar state. Bevan's centralised National Health Service and welfare state deliberately gave little or no control to local government. 'The man in Whitehall knows best' was the maxim of the post-war Fabian generation. After 1979, what was left of local independence came under sustained assault from 'control or abolish' Thatcher.

The historian Richard Tombs puts it thus:

> The growth of the state is a Europe-wide phenomenon arising from the extension of welfare democracy, but rarely in such a centralised form as in England: the proportion of our public spending controlled from the centre is roughly twice that in France, Japan and Italy, and more than three times that in Germany ... The clatter of dropped hospital bedpans, GCSE results in Norfolk, teenage stabbings in Brixton, floods in Somerset – a never-ending conveyor belt

of everyday problems – create a political and administrative burden that Whitehall and Westminster can neither manage nor surrender. Devolution of power to Edinburgh, Cardiff and Belfast has made England's position all the more stark.

This is not to argue that central government should have minimal power. Rather power should match functions and accountability. The right to make decisions should flow to the level – whether local, national or supranational – that is best able to undertake them democratically. When Tombs describes overcentralisation as 'a seventy-year habit we cannot, or will not, break', the 'we' is us in England, and the target is the hoarding of power in London. In particular, 'we' is a generation of ministers who scapegoated 'Brussels' for taking powers away from 'Britain' while resolutely refusing to share power at home with local authorities striving to tackle major social problems like housing.

The EU is a bystander to this local powerlessness within England. Insofar as it plays a role, it is a positive one: in many of Britain's poorer regions, especially in the north and west of England, EU regional development programmes have flourished precisely because they provide systematic long-term backing for local initiatives which 'their' government in London won't support. We noted in chapter 1 that the 'balance of competences' review concluded that the distribution of power between Brussels and London was broadly fair. A similar review within Britain would by contrast be ferocious about the undue concentration of power in London.

London, capital of the historically large unitary state of England since at least the twelfth century, and a Roman trading city long before, has always been by far its richest and most successful metropolis. The pool of London is where Sir Francis Drake docked the *Golden Hind* after his circumnavigation of the globe with a hold full of stolen Spanish gold – the foundation, Keynes argued, of London's financial strength. Its long-standing openness to trade and people was further boosted by generations of state support for the growth of finance in the centuries after the founding of the Bank of England in 1694.

However, it is highly significant that London is the part of England that historically has enjoyed most devolution. It has had power to capitalise on its advantages – and to steer its way through shocks and setbacks.

The historic 'square mile' of the City of London boasted its Mayor and Corporation long before Magna Carta; indeed, King John pledged that 'the City of London shall enjoy its ancient liberties'. The City of London Corporation, with its 690th Lord Mayor, remains rich and powerful, and has fought off all attempts at abolition over the centuries. For all its quaint traditions, maybe because of them, the Corporation is a remarkable force for civic virtue and self-confidence, maintaining some of London's great open spaces, including Hampstead Heath and Epping Forest, providing social housing, fostering the arts through the Barbican Centre, the London Symphony Orchestra, the Royal Shakespeare Company and the Guildhall School of Music and Drama, and promoting education through City University, the Cass Business School, the Museum of

London and the City of London's schools. The Corporation is no political innocent: it is a consistent and elegantly ruthless lobbyist for policies supporting the City and financial services. Britain's pro-City industrial strategy has part of its authorship here.

The metropolitan region of London, with a population larger than Scotland and Wales put together, had its own elected government from the Victorian era until 1986, when it was abolished by Margaret Thatcher because she wanted rid of its Labour leader Ken Livingstone. This was her second big 'control or abolish' play – the first was the undermining of devolution to Scotland and Wales on becoming Tory leader in 1975. The third was her bid to begin withdrawal from the EU with her Bruges speech of 1988.

Abolition of the Greater London Council was fiercely opposed at the time. Business leaders in the capital were soon agitating for 'something to be done', regarding a bit of municipal socialism as less harmful than a city where the trains and roads were in chaos. Accordingly, an early act of the Blair government, with business support, was to create a mayor of London.

'Ken', 'Boris' and 'Sadiq', London's three popular mayors since 2000, have significantly improved the capital's public transport. Ken and Boris also deserve great credit for the success of the 2012 London Olympics. London's thirty-three elected borough councils, which survived the abolition of the GLC and benefited from a burgeoning population, also have a creditable record since the 1990s of improving the capital's public services. Previously a byword for failure and decay,

London's infrastructure is now seen as a national and even international exemplar.

The success of London's mayoralty shows how quickly bold political leadership can transform a city and seize its imagination and loyalty. It is a model for England at large.

Mayors all round

'Control or abolish' Thatcher didn't just abolish the Greater London Council. In 1986 she also abolished England's six other principal metropolitan authorities, covering Greater Manchester, the West Midlands, Merseyside, West and South Yorkshire, and Tyne and Wear. John Major went on to abolish Humberside. These authorities had served 11 million English city dwellers, more than twice the population of Scotland, including many of England's poorest and seriously declining areas.

A semblance of self-government is being restored to some of England's city regions beyond London through 'metro mayors'. London and Manchester's success is changing the argument. Instead of suspicion of another layer of government, there is a growing demand to grasp the same opportunity. But these metro mayors are not a patch on London's.

Everyday local government in England, beneath the city region level, is everywhere starved of resources. Its independent tax base is tiny, and a decade of austerity as default national policy has slashed Whitehall funding too, as we observed earlier. Here again, this long-standing weakness in English local government was dramatically exacerbated by Thatcher's 'control or abolish' reflexes. Her last and most controversial major reform, in 1989, was to abolish the local property tax and replace it with a per capita 'poll tax', crippling the tax base even of the local authorities she did not abolish, and so making them almost totally subservient to Whitehall.

Britain is the only country in the modern world to have introduced a poll tax. Three decades later, local government still hasn't recovered. A popular revolt against the tax was one of the reasons for Thatcher's fall. However, as on Europe, her successor John Major met her halfway. He replaced it with a bastardised property tax, with the consequences we discussed in chapter 5. Also true to form, the Blair government kept this council tax largely unchanged.

A Statute of Self-Government is needed to reinvent local government in England. Every city region should have a powerful mayor with responsibility for public transport, policing, skills training, regeneration and strategic planning. More local 'district' councils should be given powers to provide new and better social housing and improved services for children, the elderly and families. To make this possible, local government needs a substantial property tax base, plus taxes transferred from Whitehall to localities. Given the stark divergence in wealth and income between England's regions, national taxation needs to equalise between poor and rich communities.

Should there be a specifically English Parliament and government? This has superficial attractions until the realities of power are considered. So dominant is England within the

United Kingdom – 85 per cent of its population and a higher proportion still of tax revenues – that it is very hard to see how UK and English governments and parliaments could coexist without one subsuming the other. The viable course, reflecting historic identities within England, is to devolve to city regions and to counties or groups of counties, and to entrench representatives of these English authorities in the new Federal Senate we propose, alongside representatives of the devolved parliaments and assemblies of Scotland, Wales and Northern Ireland. This is the way to create a federal UK.

A United and Federal Kingdom

The Great Charter should inaugurate a United and Federal Kingdom, including a Federal Senate to replace the House of Lords.

Henry VIII would recognise the outward forms of the existing House of Lords with its dukes, earls, barons and bishops. However, most of the hereditary aristocrats were removed by the Blair government in 1999, and the Lords is now largely an assembly of appointed 'life peers'. As a democratic House of Commons evolved in the twentieth century, the Lords shrivelled into a weak revising chamber, with only a marginal capacity to challenge the supremacy of the elected House.

Ministers have virtually untrammelled control of the English state by virtue of the fact that the Commons is controlled by the leaders of its majority party, who are at one and the same time both MPs and ministers directing the whole

Whitehall machine. The 'Thatcherism in one country' philosophy of the Brexiters flows from this 'elective dictatorship'. It needs to be consigned to history by a federal constitution and accompanying institutions.

A Federal Senate of the United Kingdom could be directly or indirectly elected. The US has the world's most powerful directly elected federal Senate, while Germany has a successful indirectly elected second chamber (*Bundesrat*), representing the German state governments. The *Bundesrat* could be a model for the UK. It brings the city and regional leaders from Germany's sixteen states, from Hamburg in the north to Bavaria in the south, to the German Parliament at least once a month, projecting them as national political figures on a par with ministers in Berlin.

A British version of the *Bundesrat* would convene Nicola Sturgeon, Sadiq Khan, Carwen Jones, Andy Burnham, Andy Street and Arlene Foster at least once a month, in Parliament, to debate the big issues facing their cities, nations and regions. The interaction between the directly elected *Bundestag* and the federal *Bundesrat* institutionalises power-sharing between national and devolved government in Germany. The *Bundesrat* has significant power over legislation and taxation affecting the German states, but the *Bundestag* controls national taxation and elects the Chancellor, so avoiding gridlock between the two Houses. A federal second chamber could operate in a similar way in Britain, abolishing the 'elective dictatorship'.

To symbolise and stimulate the dispersion of power across England, the Federal Senate of the United Kingdom should meet in the North of England. The location should be determined by a Constitutional Convention, along with its precise composition. The Convention should meet in the North of England in 2019, perhaps in York, where Parliament frequently assembled in the decades after Magna Carta. When the HS2 high-speed line opens from London to Birmingham and the North in the early 2030s, Manchester and Leeds will be just over an hour from London, and half an hour from Birmingham. These would be attractive and nationally accessible locations for the Federal Senate.

Parliament should learn from the monarchy, the UK's most popular state institution, which is also the one most dispersed across the United Kingdom. With unfailing annual routine the Queen progresses from Buckingham Palace and Windsor to Sandringham in Norfolk at Christmas and Balmoral in the Scottish Highlands for the summer, after holding court in the Palace of Holyroodhouse in Edinburgh. The Prince of Wales, invested in Caernarfon Castle, has an official residence in Carmarthenshire.

When the House of Commons was bombed by Hitler in 1941, Churchill insisted it be rebuilt to its historic design, with benches facing each other and not in a semicircle. 'We shape our buildings and afterwards our buildings shape us,' he said. The new Senate should be a magnificent statement of twenty-first-century Federal Britain in the North of England. Fortuitously, the Palace of Westminster is falling down and about to undergo complete renovation. This is an opportune moment for reshaping our parliamentary buildings and their occupants.

Reinventing England's cities

Our ambition is for the Great Charter, like Magna Carta, to become famous for what it starts, notably the renaissance of England's cities and city regions beyond London.

Apart from London and perhaps Birmingham and Manchester/Salford, England's cities quickly fall below the population threshold to support the full array of public and private institutions of a diversified urban economy. Wherever possible the opportunity should be taken to create city regions that are big. Scale matters: not for administrative convenience, but because it enables the city regional leaders to get the best from interlinking their urban areas, thereby boosting growth – 'agglomeration'.

Agglomeration is essential because most of England's cities are just too small. Whether it's the density of transport links, the range of healthcare or the demand needed to support company start-ups or viable cultural and sporting institutions, the international evidence is that successful cities need to serve substantial populations.

Cities, like nations, rise and fall much faster than is commonly appreciated. London's population rose more than sevenfold, from one million to seven million, in the nineteenth century. Liverpool's population halved in the thirty years after the Second World War and has barely increased since. Cambridge and its commuter belt could well become England's second city region in wealth, if not population, within another generation if the phenomenal success of its university and related industries and start-ups continues.

Oxford could follow suit. Cities like Liverpool, Cambridge and Oxford, although small by international standards, possess enough 'anchor' institutions and infrastructure for it to be conceivable that they could scale rapidly, if sufficiently supported with radically improved industrial policy and connectivity to London and their hinterlands.

Vital to the success of most English cities is a transformation in east–west connectivity, as well as improvements in rail services to London. So for Cambridge, whose rail links with London have been transformed in the past generation, a new 'brain belt' rail line is vital, going west to Bedford, Milton Keynes, Oxford, Swindon, Bath, Bristol, Cardiff and Swansea. For Liverpool, the proposed 'Crossrail of the North' going east to Manchester, Leeds, Bradford, Hull, York and Newcastle is equally important, as it is for all those cities. The distances are not great, but connectivity is woeful. The only way to get from Cambridge to Oxford by train is via London, taking three hours and multiple changes, while the train called the Trans-Pennine Express takes an hour to cover forty miles from Manchester to Leeds, so qualifying for mis-selling under the Trade Descriptions Act. Connectivity is a huge issue across the UK. Left-behind Britain is not just isolated by poverty and lack of opportunity; it is also left behind by poor transport links, particularly to and from London, the heart of the national economy. This is not a matter so much of distance as infrastructure. Lincoln, only 156 miles from London, takes three hours to reach from the capital, involving at least one change. Weymouth in Dorset, geographically closer to London (142 miles) than is Liverpool (196 miles) takes far longer to reach by train. International evidence is that the more geographical mobility, the greater social mobility.

These challenges of regional connectivity would rightly be top of the agenda for the new Federal Senate meeting in one of the northern cities so poorly networked at present. Digital connectivity – superfast broadband and 4G mobile coverage – is also deplorably bad. Mayors are far better placed to sort out such issues than distant and unbriefed ministers and quangos in Whitehall.

Cities like Bradford and Sunderland, overshadowed by nearby larger cities (Leeds and Newcastle in their cases), face still more acute problems. Worst-placed are the isolated small cities and large towns, such as Hull, Blackpool and Barnsley, which suffer a toxic combination of isolation, depopulation and deindustrialisation. They all need credible industrial strategies shaped by strong civic leaders. Ask the leader of any of England's city councils what is the biggest challenge facing their locality, and almost invariably the reply is about cuts in Whitehall grants. What's needed instead is a transformational agenda for jobs, infrastructure and quality of life, city by city and region by region.

Imagine. While the House of Commons considers national taxation, immigration policy, relations with Putin's Russia and British leadership in the European Union, the Federal Senate would simultaneously be in session, addressing the imperative for HS3, for a University of Peterborough, the plans for a Swansea Tidal Barrage, Blackpool's Strategy for a Green Energy Revolution, at the behest of their mayors and regional leaders. This would be a fundamental improvement in the government of Britain, which presently has almost no sub-national government worth the name.

Returning to Lincoln, the small but magnificent and historic city just mentioned. Two decades ago its leaders recognised the need for radical change. The city lacked a higher education institution, and the council's original plan was to attract a satellite campus. But bold leadership, enlisting EU and development funding of £200 million, led to the creation of a successful regional university that now has thirteen thousand students and 1350 staff, including the UK's first purpose-built engineering school in twenty-five years, developed in collaboration with the German engineering giant Siemens, which had considered leaving the area. The university has brought self-confidence and economic benefit: it is a city teeming with students and life. Not every small city can build a great university, but every small city can have a great plan for something just as good.

The renaissance of England's cities would be boosted by Parliament voting to relocate more public institutions to cities outside London. There is no good reason for the Supreme Court to be located in Parliament Square. Why not Norwich, Exeter or Chester, historic cities with ancient courts of law? Channel Four recently fought off proposals for it to be relocated outside London; this decision should be revisited. Far more of the BBC, including news and drama, should move north to Salford, which has been a great success as the BBC's secondary location since 2004.

'More democracy'

'The cure for the ailments of democracy is more democracy,' said the American social reformer John Dewey in his book *The Public and Its Problems* (1927), which helped pave the way for Franklin Delano Roosevelt and his New Deal in the 1930s.

Dewey would say the same of Britain and its problems today, and the answer to them too is more democracy to instil hope, passion and ambition for change. Clement Attlee, a British contemporary of FDR, said that democracy was 'government by discussion'. We need more, not less discussion, on the big issues, including Europe. The worst argument against a people's vote (referendum) on the Brexit deal is that it will be 'divisive' and prolong a national argument. Better, on all big issues, to have prolonged argument than prolonged tragedy.

Vital to democracy and citizenship is having the vote and using it. Young people, hugely concerned and energised by Brexit, are demanding the right to be heard. Since the 1960s the young have taken a back seat in our national conversation. A century after the Suffragettes secured the vote for women, it is time for the next democratic advance: giving sixteen- and seventeen-year-olds the vote.

The UK Youth Parliament argues persuasively for lowering the voting age. Their case is unanswerable by any but the same old tawdry arguments against greater democracy down the ages. Participation by sixteen- and seventeen-year-olds had a positive effect on the independence debate in Scotland. Both Scotland and Wales have now lowered the voting age for their elections, and many other countries worldwide have either done so or are considering it.

Young people are engaging in politics in record numbers, and not just because of Brexit. After a decade of neglect, the young are 'taking back real control'. They know they have paid the price of thinking that politics was irrelevant: a decade when university tuition fees trebled and apprenticeship numbers went down, while pensioners – who voted – got big real increases in their basic income through the 'triple lock' on the state pension, as well as clinching the vote for Brexit.

The vote should be conferred on sixteen- and seventeen-year-olds as part of a 'youth democracy' package including four other elements: automatic voter registration of all teenagers in their place of study; a ballot box in every secondary school, college and university on polling day; citizenship GCSE as a compulsory part of England's national curriculum; and mandatory voting for all sixteen- to twenty-one-year-olds in general elections and referendums. Taken together, this 'youth democracy' reform will make citizenship a rite of passage for British teenagers, a fundamental social change for the better. Research shows that people who vote in the first election for which they are eligible very largely vote in elections thereafter; it becomes a habit and expectation, as it should be in a civilisation of liberty.

Compulsory voting for sixteen- to twenty-one-year-olds is a bold but necessary element. Australia has mandatory voting; making it mandatory in Britain for under-21s to vote, while also making it highly convenient to do so in their place of study, should be the 'citizenship deal' for the young. A great

innovation of recent years, although greeted with some cyni-
cism in the liberal media, was the introduction of citizenship
tests and ceremonies for immigrants taking UK citizenship. It
is high time we did the same for British teenagers too, as they
assume the privileges and responsibilities of citizenship.

Once sixteen- and seventeen-year-olds have the vote,
Parliament and parliamentary – and local council – candidates
will treat them, and young people at large, with a new serious-
ness. Instead of schools often being closed on polling days so
that the 'adults' can use them to vote, schools will themselves
become hubs of democracy. Election candidates will be desperate to hold hustings in schools to appeal to the 'youth vote',
in the same way they now routinely visit homes for the elderly.

A big boost should also be given to National Citizen Service
(NCS), the only offspring of David Cameron's 'big society'.
Teenagers of all backgrounds should be encouraged – and
be given bursaries if they can't afford it – to engage in NCS
during the summer after they leave school, as another rite of
passage to citizenship. There should be one condition: that
NCS is undertaken in a part of the UK some distance from
where the young person lives, so that teenagers discover more
about their own country. It would be great if the Republic of
Ireland joined NCS, so that British teenagers could volunteer
in Ireland and vice versa. (The authors' profits from this book
are going to 'Europe awards' for teenagers to study or volunteer in the EU; this could be done as part of NCS.)

The armed forces should play a big part in National Citizen
Service and should offer a hundred thousand places a year for
teenagers to undertake at least two months of service, including

opportunities to train on the European mainland. Britain will never be 'one nation' until there is far more solidarity between young people of all backgrounds and parts of the country.

This stronger approach to rights and responsibilities is required across the board – vital to tackling our social crisis. The Human Rights Act of 1998, which enshrined the post-war European Convention on Human Rights into British law, is almost entirely about basic civil rights to freedom from state violence and oppression. These are vital liberties. But the Convention has little to say about social, economic and environmental rights, beyond an undefined 'right to education', and less still about social obligations. Integral to the Great Charter, there should be a British Statute of Social Rights and Responsibilities which enshrines them. No constitution can wave a magic wand, but it can help hold those in power to a high standard of duty, and create expectations that citizens too will act on their responsibilities. These are advantages to be prized.

The enumerated rights in the Statute of Social Rights and Responsibilities should include a right to education or training until at least the age of twenty-one; a right to protection against maltreatment for children, the infirm and the disabled; a right to decent healthcare; a right to decent housing; a right to an environment which is sustainable, unpolluted and not harmful to health and wellbeing; and a right to fair employment practices. These mirror the EU's new 'Pillar of Social Rights'.

As for duties, every citizen of the United Kingdom should have a duty to nurture and protect their children; a duty to vote and to do jury service; a duty for children to care for their elderly parents so far as they are able; a duty to protect the environment; and a duty on all independent adults to maintain themselves financially so far as they are able. These would be declaratory duties; legal offences would only flow from specific laws designating crimes, as now.

Liberal sceptics may consider this 'motherhood and apple pie', while the neo-liberal right will shriek 'nanny state' and bluster about Brexit. But echoing Ben Okri we want a constitution that tells 'the best story about ourselves to ourselves', which must surely include the best story of how we treat each other. The first sentence of the Statute of Rights and Responsibilities should be: 'There is such a thing as society, of which all citizens are equal members.'

The media should not be exempt from 'rights and responsibilities'. Just as freedom of expression is enshrined in the Human Rights Act, so should the responsibility to respect the privacy of citizens who are not public figures and to maintain standards of honesty and impartiality in the reporting of news. Britain's tradition of public-service broadcasting ensures that TV and radio provide information that is balanced, fair and true, even if there are falls from grace.

When the BBC reporter Brian Hanrahan said that he had counted the jump jets out and back on the aircraft carrier *Hermes* during an attack on Port Stanley in the Falklands war, and none had been shot down as the Argentines claimed, everyone in the world believed him. The BBC strayed from this gold standard over the specially divisive issue of Brexit, where impartiality has been interpreted as giving excessive time to extremists, particularly Nigel Farage, while failing properly to evaluate key factual assertions. We want the BBC to improve not to wither – it remains the best we have.

Impartiality rules should also apply to Britain's written media and social media companies. Research has found that fake news spreads faster on Twitter than does real news. Fake news stories are 70 per cent more likely to be retweeted than true stories, and it takes six times longer for true stories to reach any 1500 people than it does for fabrications. Serious data breaches at Facebook and Cambridge Analytica, allowing the mass profiling of users for political campaigning, are not only a fundamental breach of privacy but a grave threat to the future of democracy. Every citizen should own their own data as a twenty-first-century constitutional right.

Last but not least of the components of the Great Charter for Modern Britain is our proposed treaty commitment to engage fully in the European Union. This is vital for the flourishing of both Britain and Europe – convinced, as the Treaty of Paris put it so eloquently, that 'the contribution which an organised and vital Europe can make to civilisation is indispensable to the maintenance of peaceful relations'.

7

Statues of liberty

Belgrade's Commission for Monuments and Naming of Streets and Squares is considering – as we write – erecting a statue of Slobodan Miloševi, the Serbian dictator who twenty years ago carried out mass murder and genocide in Croatia, Bosnia and Kosovo.

Miloševi is a war criminal on a par with those hanged in Nuremberg and Tokyo in 1946. It would be the equivalent of a statue of Hitler in Berlin. Yet a substantial body of Serbs now see him as a national hero. His monument is being promoted by the youth wing of his Socialist Party, back in power in Belgrade, whose members are too young to have witnessed his crimes against humanity.

The Miloševi statue is part of a wave of authoritarian and nationalist counter-revolution now threatening Europe. In the six decades of the EU, no EU member state has invaded another, and none has yet disowned democracy, remarkable achievements for a Europe which in the previous six decades was ravaged by two wars of medieval ferocity and destruction.

But the past is never fully overcome; we can't even be sure that its worst horrors are over. Echoes of the years before 1914, and the 1930s, ring louder. Brexiters who dismiss them as alarmist do so from ignorance or self-delusion.

Counter-revolution

Sir Ivor Roberts, British ambassador to Miloševi 's Belgrade and Berlusconi's Rome, writes of the growing European crisis:

> There is a clear fault line running from Belgrade to Budapest and Warsaw. The new division is between those who believe that their best hope for peace and prosperity lies in joining the rules-based European Union and NATO and those who base their hopes on the pursuit of nationalism and authoritarianism. The nationalists bridle at the demands the EU makes and prefer the Moscow model – governments headed by strong men, supported by more strong men.

Vladimir Putin's gangster nationalism is a contemporary form of fascism. His twenty-year reign has seen Russian democracy grow vestigial. The duma is little more than a puppet, with the security apparatus inherited from the Soviet Union assuming ever more untrammelled power. Corporations have been built with state sponsorship, conferring vast wealth and power on loyal cronies, who know that the penalty for anything less than unwavering loyalty is to be jailed indefinitely on trumped-up charges, hunted down and even murdered if they defect. One Russian law-enforcement agency has, as its coat of arms, a bunch of the same *fascii* as in the emblem of the Italian Fascist Party, in the claws of a double-headed eagle.

'We are in a new era,' warns Madeleine Albright, the former US Secretary of State, 'testing whether the democratic banner can remain aloft amid terrorism, sectarian conflicts, vulnerable borders, rogue social media and the cynical schemes of ambitious men.' She sees in Europe and beyond 'the tendencies that lead toward fascism', which 'pose a more serious threat now than at any time since the end of World War II'. Putin boasts constantly that the imperial USSR that disintegrated in the 1980s and 1990s was 'the same Russia, just called by a different name'. 'Russia makes little secret of the fact that it will do what it takes to ensure the Orthodox countries of former Yugoslavia do not join NATO,' says Ivor Roberts. Hence the clumsy attempt by Russian agents to assassinate Milo Đjukanovi , former President of Montenegro, Serbia's south-eastern neighbour, to prevent him from leading his little Balkan country into NATO in 2016, and equally crude attempts to prevent Zoran Zaev from taking power from the pro-Russian nationalists in Macedonia, Serbia's southern neighbour, in 2017.

Counter-revolution is equally virulent in central and eastern Europe. Hungary's Viktor Orbán, the young liberal hero of 1989, now praises Putin, Xi Jinping, Erdo an and Trump. He is not seeking to leave the EU – Hungary is its biggest per capita aid recipient and it is hugely popular. But Orbán's model for Europe is less a union of democracies, more a reincarnation of the authoritarian Concert of Europe masterminded by the ruthlessly reactionary early nineteenth-century chancellor of the Austro-Hungarian empire, Prince Metternich.

Virtually every country in Europe now contains parties on the counter-revolutionary spectrum, including UKIP, whose Nigel Farage is an avowed admirer of Putin. 'Is Europe disintegrating? Can an open society survive? How is the economic crisis to be overcome? Will Europeans feel secure again?' asks the Polish historian Jan Zielonka in his 2018 book *Counter-Revolution: Liberal Europe in Retreat.* He is not optimistic about the likely answers: 'Today the entirety of Europe is in a state of confusion with the liberal system beginning to crumble not just in Warsaw and Budapest but also in London, Amsterdam, Madrid, Rome, Athens, and Paris.' He is especially scathing about Europe's leaders, who 'look incompetent and dishonest'.

Timothy Garton Ash, chronicler of Poland's suffering under communism, is astonished at how Europe has degenerated in barely a decade:

Had I been cryogenically frozen in 2005, I would have gone to my provisional rest as a happy European. The capitals of Europe felt as if they were bathed in sunlight from windows newly opened in ancient dark palaces. The periphery of Europe was apparently converging with the continent's historic core. Young Spaniards, Greeks, Poles, and Portuguese spoke optimistically about the new chances offered them by Europe. Even notoriously eurosceptical Britain was embracing its European future under Tony Blair.

Now, however, 'cryogenically reanimated, I would imme-diately have died again from shock, for now there is crisis and disintegration wherever I look'. Putin's seizure of Crimea and subversion of Ukraine, in particular, are 'actions recalling Europe in 1939 rather than 1989'.

Tony Judt concluded his magisterial history of Europe since 1945, *Postwar*, published in 2005, with boldly optimistic words: 'Few would have predicted it sixty years before, but the twenty-first century might yet belong to Europe.' The twenty-first century is now in danger of belonging to pop-ulists branding independent judges 'ENEMIES OF THE PEOPLE': the headline in the *Daily Mail* denouncing the UK Supreme Court, no less, who dared to rule that Parliament must have a vote on Brexit.

By 'the people', populists don't mean 'all the people', but just those who agree with them. As Garton Ash puts it:

when Nigel Farage welcomed the Brexit vote as a vic-tory for 'ordinary people', 'decent people', and 'real people', the 48 percent of us who voted on June 23, 2016, for Britain to remain in the EU are plainly neither ordinary nor decent, nor even real. Everywhere it's the 'other people' who now have to watch out: Mexicans and Muslims in the US, Kurds in Turkey, Poles in Britain, Muslims and Jews all over Europe, as well as Sinti and Roma, refugees, immigrants, black people, women, cosmopolitans, homosexuals, not to mention 'experts', 'elites', and 'mainstream media'.

The language Putin understands is force and power, yet at this critical time the West conveys generally weak, contradictory signals, starting with Trump. The West appears scarcely present in much of the former Yugoslavia. EU membership is a receding chimera for Serbia, abandoned to the Russian bear. Ukraine, a huge state between Poland and Russia, occupying the entire north shore of the Black Sea opposite Turkey, is desperately precarious. Its southern province of Crimea was annexed by Putin; its eastern provinces ravaged by thugs let loose by Moscow. Putin's policy is obvious: suzerainty over as much of Eastern Europe and former Soviet Central Asia as he can achieve, while destabilising the West at large.

Pause to consider the magnitude of Russia's violation of Ukraine. A decade ago Ukraine, an ancient European civilisation, was courting membership of both the EU and NATO. Then, in a fascist-style coup from central casting, an army of 'little green men' laden with Russian equipment invaded Crimea. While the West argued in the United Nations about the provenance of these 'polite people', as the Russian media dubbed them, they had overrun the Black Sea peninsula's defence installations. Whereupon Putin intervened to 'restore order', as Russian-trained troops and auxiliaries in parallel spread chaos across eastern Ukraine and destabilised Kiev politically. As a dystopian saga, it would stretch credulity. It happened in our Europe, in our decade.

Crimea is the first invasion and annexation of a European state since the Second World War. It is hard to be confident that it will be the last. Russian troops are massed on the borders of the three small Baltic states, whose Russian minorities are being stirred up in textbook nationalist fashion. Lithuania, the westernmost of the Baltics, borders Poland, which borders Germany. An increasingly worried Berlin, still weak and uncertain militarily, for all its economic might commanding only a fraction of Moscow's military capacity, is entirely dependent upon NATO for protection and deterrence. Germany and the rest of mainland Europe should spend more on defence, but a semi-detached Britain is hardly best placed to persuade them.

Forces of liberalism are depleted but resisting, including in Ukraine and the Balkans. In Ukraine, an Association Agreement with the EU formally came into effect in 2017 – a thin but important lifeline. In Macedonia, the charismatic Zoran Zaev, having survived the Putin-inspired putsch, is winning support for his anti-nationalist message of reconciliation with Greece and civic equality, and joining NATO and the EU. Even within the Serbian Socialist Party, there are pro-Western and pro-EU voices. Miloševi 's statue is not yet erected. A pivotal struggle is raging to contain Putin and his 'polite people'.

Resistance to Russian proto-fascism and the protection of European democracy are critical British interests and values. A central argument running through this book is that the dispute between Brexit and anti-Brexit, between an isolationist and an engaged view of Britain in Europe, harks back to Churchill and Chamberlain's great dispute of 1938. Was Germany's threat to Czechoslovakia, in Chamberlain's words, 'a quarrel in a faraway country between people of whom we know nothing'? Or was it an existential threat to Britain's own security and democracy, as Churchill argued? We have no equivocation whatever in siding with Churchill, and we set out his conviction of how Britain must place itself in Europe in chapter 3.

Today's Churchill–Chamberlain argument is crystallising into a specific and urgent issue: is NATO alone enough to maintain the long-term security of Europe and Britain?

It's not just NATO, stupid

The stock response – usually the only response – of Brexiters to Europe's crisis of security and democracy is 'NATO'. As we are staying in NATO, peace and security will be okay and it is scaremongering to suggest otherwise. NATO and the transatlantic alliance are strong and solid enough to be the sole institutional bulwarks against Russia and the threat to democratic forces across Europe. Keep calm and carry on.

However, 'It's NATO, stupid' doesn't wash. In the first place, NATO is only one part of Europe's security system as it has developed since the Second World War. Also important is the formal and informal machinery of the EU. Constant dialogue between governments takes place in the Council of Ministers, particularly the regular meetings of heads of governments and foreign ministers, where discussions 'in the margins', and in parallel committees of officials, are as important to building solidarity as formal ministerial sessions. When a hundred Russian intelligence officers across Europe were expelled after the Salisbury attack in March 2018, in support of Britain, it followed a meeting of the European Council in Brussels whose communiqué was toughened after a robust presentation by Theresa May to fellow heads of government.

Of the EU twenty-seven, only France is a permanent member of the United Nations Security Council. Germany, Italy, Sweden and the Netherlands are not. Exclusion from the EU can only weaken Britain's voice and engagement with the major European states on security and defence.

NATO itself is far from secure, with twenty-nine members, many of them small central and east European states admitted in the halcyon days after the collapse of the Berlin Wall, when it looked as if Russia itself might join the West too. NATO's performance in Afghanistan and Libya has been dire. Its north European front is constituted by the small and petrified Baltic statelets; its southern flank is Turkey, whose Putinesque leader Erdo an is alarming NATO leaders not only by his own version of authoritarian megalomania but, more practically and deliberately, by buying missile defence systems from Russia which cannot be used against them.

Then there is Donald Trump, who as a candidate lambasted NATO as obsolete and equivocated in his endorsement of Article 5, the critical NATO mutual-defence commitment. General Petr Pavel, chairman of NATO's military committee and the first East European to hold the role, says that Europe needs to 'grow up' and be willing to 'provide all the capabilities to handle a regional crisis without American engagement, if the US does not wish to engage'. Such uncertainty about US commitment would have been unthinkable during the last Cold War against Russia. Now it is the conversation at every NATO and European security meeting. Trump initially declined even to criticise Putin over the Salisbury attack and his appointment in April 2018 of 'America first and only' unilateralists, Mike Pompeo and John Bolton as Secretary of State and National Security Advisor respectively, is another warning signal. Bolton, a prime mover behind George W. Bush's invasion of Iraq, has no time for 'EUroids', as he calls us in his embittered memoirs. His particular bête noire is the Obama–European-brokered nuclear agreement with Iran, an EU foreign policy success now in jeopardy.

However, there is a more fundamental problem with 'It's NATO, stupid'. Countries that engage in trade wars and economic disputes are less likely to unite over common defence and security. Long before Anglo-German military rivalry blew up in war in 1914, Britain and Germany engaged in bitter trade wars, including industrial espionage, as Bismarck's newly unified Germany sought successfully to challenge Britain's fading economic predominance. It didn't help that Kaiser Wilhelm II was unstable and aggressive. But the unstable and aggressive are often in charge of great nations: enter Trump, Putin, Erdoan. At present France and German, in the hands of reliable rationalists Macron and Merkel, are firm and predictable allies. But in the shifting world of today's geo and domestic politics, to bet that France and Germany will always be strong and stable is the ultimate triumph of hope over experience.

It is vital to understand that one historic option is ruled out for Britain in the foreseeable future, namely a renewal of the balance of power diplomacy in Europe. This was English then British policy from the rise of modern European nation states in the sixteenth century until the end of the Second World War.

For those four hundred years England sided with – and sometimes formed – European coalitions including either France or Germany, depending on which of them held the upper hand on the mainland and threatened England. So as England we lined up with Germans against Louis XIV; then as Britain with Germans, Austrians, Spanish, Portuguese and Russians against Napoleon; but with France, and Russia too when it was so minded, against Hitler and the Kaiser.

In the era of the European Union, unlikely to end any time soon, there are no 'divide and rule' or 'balance of power' options for Britain to exploit in Europe. For it is within the EU, not outside it, that Europe's modern states form their alliances, broker their deals and engage in balance of power politics – for good or ill. All four living ex-prime ministers (two Tory, two Labour) know this and worked tirelessly to create alliances within the EU for British objectives, including for our successive opt-outs, budget rebates and wider international objectives, notably African development, free trade, climate change and response to the financial crash. It is why they all favour staying in the EU, without equivocation. Ironically, the prime minister who succeeded best at steering the EU from inside was Margaret Thatcher with the single market, until, faced with the 'socialist' Jacques Delors as Commission President, she decided – as described in chapter 2 – to destroy rather than build, and gave up on diplomacy. A top aide to Chancellor Merkel told one of the authors that Britain is abandoning the very institutions from which it was shaping Europe in its own image.

For Brexit Britain, the binary choice in most circumstances will simply be one of seeking 'good' or 'bad' relations with mainland Europe as a whole. No more capacity to play off France against Germany, or vice versa, with the Dutch and/or the Swedes as allies. Jacob Rees-Mogg celebrated the triggering of Article 50 (to give notice to leave the EU) by comparing Theresa May to 'Gloriana' – Elizabeth I, the subtle mistress of European balance of power politics, and never the prey of her court. If only.

British policy should be to have the closest possible relations with the EU in the face not only of Putin's Russia, but also Xi's China, Trump's America, the mullahs' Iran, and a chronically unstable Middle East and North Africa, as well as global environmental and social threats that observe no borders. China's President Xi represents a threat which, in the long term, may be greater even than Russia's. Having abolished term limits to become president for life, Xi is now more in control of the Chinese Communist Party than any leader since Mao, and is slowing down the pace of market-oriented reforms. He has introduced the 'social credit system' through which the Chinese government will assign a rating to every Chinese citizen based on this data – the most complete system of Orwellian social control ever devised.

An increasingly hostile participant in the international order, which Xi regards as a construct of the victors of the twentieth century, he is calling for a 'new type of international system' and trading blows in a potential trade war with US. He is fostering counterweights to the US and Europe with the Asian Infrastructure Investment Bank, the Shanghai Cooperation Organization and his 'Belt and Road Initiative', to create a dedicated Chinese-led Asian economic and political axis. For Britain to attempt to negotiate with China on our own, as a middle-sized power divorced from the EU, is – as we saw in chapter 4 – to go swimming with crocodiles.

By far the best way for Britain to confront these international challenges is from the heart of the EU. The only questions if we depart are how much it weakens our security, and how far we can limit the damage. Plainly we cannot predict the future any more than our forebears could in the years leading up to 1914 and 1939. But the risks of diplomatic frailty, rivalrous trade relationships, weakening the EU, and sending nervous, inconsistent messages to Putin, Trump and Xi are considerable. They are already being felt.

Never underestimate how fast instability and threats can turn to outright crisis and war. A week before the outbreak of the First World War in August 1914, Prime Minister Asquith wrote to his lover about the warlike manoeuvres on the continent since the assassination of Austrian Archduke Franz Ferdinand by a nationalist terrorist in Bosnia: 'we are within measurable, or imaginable, distance of a real Armageddon'. He added: 'Happily there seems no reason why we should be anything more than spectators.' History judged otherwise.

Achilles heel

Nor should history reassure us about Ireland. 'We can't pretend it didn't happen' is the blunt verdict of conservative historian and journalist Simon Heffer. For however versed you are in Irish history, the retelling makes it no less awful, particularly the callous mistreatment of Ireland by Britain time and again until the peace process in Northern Ireland of the last thirty years.

Ireland was a colony, not a kingdom, throughout British rule. It had a so-called Parliament before the formal legislative union of 1800, but only Protestants were allowed to sit in it, and it could only discuss policy approved by Westminster. Irish trade and all essential matters pertaining to land and religion were determined in London to the benefit of England and the Anglo-Irish elite, at the expense of the native Irish.

Simon Heffer is honest and uncompromising in his summary of modern Irish history. After 1600, he writes, 'the Anglo-Irish story becomes one of a series of rebellions, uprisings and savage punishments. Each time there was destabilisation in England, Ireland seized the opportunity to assert itself. Ireland needed a war of independence before it could rule itself, and a civil war before it could be at ease with itself.'

Éamon de Valera, sentenced to death by British court martial after the Easter Rising of 1916 but reprieved because of his US citizenship, only died in 1973. His picture is everywhere in the Dáil. Micheál Martin, current leader of de Valera's Fianna Fáil ('Soldiers of Destiny') Party, has a youthful portrait of the Republic's founder behind his desk – 'the only one I have found of him half-smiling, before they tried to shoot him', the affable and pro-British Martin says. He then lays into Brexit and the dangers it poses to his nation, which today asks nothing more than the closest harmony and engagement with Britain in Europe.

Heffer ends on a happier note – 'The recent reciprocal visits of the Queen to Ireland and President Higgins to Britain suggest that a relationship of equals is possible.' But here again, Brexit is a gang plank into thin air. Common membership of the European Union since 1973 has been vital to the recent era of Anglo-Irish friendship and peace in Northern Ireland. The Good Friday Agreement of 1998 is an international treaty, pledging an open border in Ireland, power-sharing between unionists and nationalists in Northern Ireland, and institutions of co-operation between the Irish and British states, under-pinned by the EU.

Northern Ireland's power-sharing executive is, as we write in mid-2018, suspended. Ulster's nationalists are thus entirely unrepresented in their own Northern Irish government or the Westminster Parliament. For Britain to push the pres-ent unstable situation into crisis by the threat of a hard Irish border with divergent customs and regulatory regimes would be unconscionable.

Supported by the EU, Irish Taoiseach Leo Varadkar secured a key December 2017 commitment from the UK that there would be 'full regulatory alignment' between Northern Ireland and the Republic. This was conceded reluctantly by Mrs May and questioned at once and in public by David Davis and Boris Johnson. Notwithstanding their criticism it was enshrined in legal text in March 2018, and includes a back-stop provision for the continued application of EU law within Northern Ireland for at least the 'implementation' period of the twenty-one months after Brexit.

The question is now stark. What is the 'implementation period' implementing? If there can't be 'regulatory divergence' between Dublin and Belfast in the implementation period, because it breaches the Good Friday and December 2017 agreements, how can it happen thereafter? The answer is that it can't, unless there is to be a border in the Irish Sea, breaking up the single market of the United Kingdom, or unless there is indeed to be a four-hundred-mile hard border engraved across Ireland itself.

The Brexiters know this. It is why Boris Johnson, in defiance of his public statements, minuted Mrs May privately about the need to contemplate a hard border – but no worries, 'only' 5 per cent of goods would need to be searched and trucks stopped. It is also, astoundingly and dangerously, why the Brexit right has started calling for the end of the Good Friday Agreement – control or abolish, always the autocrat's mantra. A former Tory Northern Ireland Secretary and radical Brexiter, Owen Paterson, asserted that the Agreement had 'run its course', while Daniel Hannan, a Tory MEP, said that the Agreement was 'the consequence not the cause of peace'.

There were fifty terrorist deaths in Northern Ireland in the year the Agreement was signed, so that statement is chilling in its naivety and irresponsibility. Rees-Mogg has gone further backward still – and called for a neo-colonial timewarp. Ireland, he says, should leave the EU, the customs union and the single market because Britain is doing so, as if the last century, or maybe the last five centuries, were bubbles to be popped.

Ireland may become the Achilles heel of Brexit. It is shocking that this should be happening not only after the Good Friday Agreement but amidst a generation of Irish politicians who are the most pro-British ever, in one of the few European countries barely touched by the populist virus. Sinn Féin is finding it hard to make electoral headway in the Republic of Ireland ... yet.

While Britain imposes Brexit on Ireland in 2019, Ireland is holding a referendum to legalise abortion, having three years ago legalised same-sex marriage, ignoring last-gasp opposition from the Catholic hierarchy. So just as Ireland is executing a historically remarkable 'full regulatory alignment' with Britain on social policy, Britain is debating precisely how far it is going to dealign with its western neighbour. The words 'tragedy', 'Ireland' and 'Britain', so often shackled together in the past, may not have lost their kinship.

To conclude

'We have many theories of European integration, but practically none of European disintegration,' observes Jan Zielonka. It's about time we had one, because the threat of disintegration has increased, is increasing, and ought to be diminished.

Brexiters say that we must respect the 'instruction from the people' of 23 June 2016 – an oracle that they alone have the power to interpret. This is the people's choice for all time, a one-day snapshot before which we must genuflect unquestioningly, and 'get behind' whatever the cost. We contest that view of democracy.

Democracy is an ongoing process of deliberation and debate, adjusting decisions, laws and policies to circumstances, evidence and changing opinion. Brexiters' insist that the 2016 referendum decision – taken before China's reversion to dictatorship, Putin's newest campaign of lies and murder, Trump's election and the unfolding of 'America First', the consequent darkening of the international order and the confounding of the proposition that Britain can have all the benefits of the EU without being a member – can never be revisited. This demands that we abandon thinking in response to new evidence. A strength of democracy is that it allows decisions to be revisited. In disowning it, Brexiters declare themselves way outside British democratic traditions.

Too many who have deep reservations about Brexit have suspended their doubts. It may be wrong, they reflect in public and private, but we must make the best of a bad job, try to make it work and avoid the 'divisiveness' of another vote.

This defeatism misinterprets the vote. Brexit won a majority above all because the status quo was insupportable for too many people, their fears further inflamed by the threat of unstoppable immigration that could and should have been addressed. They wanted to vote against 'the system' in the UK, but the only question on the ballot paper was: 'Should the United Kingdom remain a member of the European Union or leave the European Union?'

Brexit is not going to make Britain better by doubling down on Thatcherism and austerity. The radical right trails a litany of mistakes and disasters. The radicalism that briefly looked economically successful in the 1980s and 1990s turns out to have feet of clay, generating inequalities and a degraded capitalism that has brought our country to its current pass. It is through their policies that so many fare so badly. It is this same mindset that is taking us out of the EU, in thrall to a sectarian ideology and an emotional attachment to a lost and largely imagined past. There will be a greater divisiveness in not revisiting a decision that is so palpably wrong and damaging.

We are not uncritical friends of the EU. Institutions always need improvement. More can and should be done to reconnect the EU to European citizens. In particular, national parliaments should be directly represented in Brussels to better connect national politicians – far more prominent and credible to their voters than most MEPs – with the EU. One way of doing this would be to replace half or so of MEPs with representatives from the parliaments of member states. This would help bridge the 'democratic deficit' in Brussels more effectively than any amount of EU public relations.

Equally, at a time of rising right-wing populism and anti-EU sentiment across the continent, the EU should be determinedly proactive in giving mainstream parties ammunition to fight back. Freedom of movement should be qualified by countries possessing the right to invoke short-term 'emergency breaks' if immigration reaches predefined upper thresholds. At the same time the EU must become an aggressive upholder of the great democratic values that sustain it, an enemy of right-wing nativist populism everywhere in Europe.

Those who embrace Britain's European destiny should, we believe, unite around the proposition that there be a peoples' vote on the terms of the Brexit deal. If we reject the deal, we withdraw our Article 50 notice, stay in the EU, and play our part in the leadership of Europe. But the argument must be about more than the necessity of staying. It must be buttressed by a commitment to repurpose our capitalism, reforge our social contract, and recast our democratic institutions so that they work for everyone. This will best be done against a background of rising living standards and economic growth, secured by preserving and building on our trade relationships with the EU and all the dozens of signatories to its trade deals. The economic shock of Brexit is gravely underestimated.

An appeal to European values is the foundation of a coalition that extends across society and political parties. The brave Conservatives prepared to challenge their rampant Brexit right wing are adherents of those values as much as the best of the Labour, Lib Dem, Green and Scottish Nationalist parties.

Country must be put before party. Those on the right can be assured that the EU has not prevented the UK from having the most lightly regulated labour market in the EU – while those on the left can be likewise assured that if they win a general election every commitment made in Labour's 2017 manifesto is implementable within the EU. The EU does not by treaty intrude into the National Health Service; the taxation of income, capital and corporations; education; pensions or welfare and other benefits. The UK controls more than 98 per cent of its public expenditure.

The EU is an association of nation states for common purposes, and it is by historical standards a very good one. The whole of the 'Brussels bureaucracy', that supposed fountain of red tape, is smaller than London's Metropolitan Police. The real yardage of words is contained in thousands of pages of laboriously negotiated trade treaties from which we benefit hugely.

The EU is not a superstate but promotes wide benefits for its member nation states in three key pillars – trade and competition, defence and security, and monetary/fiscal/currency integration. Britain has opted out of the last pillar, and is not on the hook for any bailout/transfers in the Eurozone. It should nonetheless play its full part in the first two. Nor does this mean signing up for a European army. European defence collaboration, needed in or out of the EU because of exploding costs, supports NATO, with all member states' defence budgets under national control. In the face of Russia, China and Trump's America, Europe, needs to be on permanent alert.

We must come together across the political spectrum and campaign to defeat Brexit – for the best future and for the nobility of a cause integral to our nationhood. Britain is part of Europe, and we should play our part in the institutions of modern Europe. Brexiters conduct the argument as if we can walk away from the EU and it will remain there, able to handle its own problems, conflicts, tensions and dissensions without us. But weakness, let alone collapse, in the EU and Eurozone would be catastrophic for Britain.

For the last forty-five years Britain has been a vital part of the alchemy that made Europe work. We are part of today's European decision-making: striking the bargains, feeling our way to a common and credible vision of our continent's future. By opting out we destabilise it and diminish ourselves.

Today's international order is not pledged by fate to continue; it has to be worked for, maintained and at times fought for. The EU is a crucial part of the power balance that sustains it, a countervailing force to secure the common global good in the face of Russia's, China's and the US's ambitions. Today's young people, and future generations, will bitterly reproach us for not being part of it.

Brexit, presented as a reversion to the great glories of British history, is in truth the opposite – a dismal retreat. Brexiters talk of a global Britain. In truth the only path to a global Britain is through Global Europe, currently being forged by the EU in its extensive trade deals and international policy.

They invoke the Commonwealth as its instrument. This farcical notion is summed up by the Director of the Institute of Commonwealth Studies, Philip Murphy, in a new book entitled *The Empire's New Clothes: The Myth of the Commonwealth.*

Britain has always been part of Europe. We helped defend it from foreign predators – the Turks in their time, and in the last century the Soviet Union – and played a central role in preventing it, just, from devouring itself between 1914 and 1945. As the historian Brendan Simms has written, we risk 'a fragmented, fearful and vulnerable Europe … less capable of delivering the economic and political stability of the continent on which not only Britain's prosperity but also her security has always depended'.

Certainly we must urgently redress our home-made economic and social problems. But these facts stand. Mrs May says of Brexit that 'a bad deal is worse than no deal'. But in truth, any deal or no deal are both worse than staying in the EU.

In *War and Peace*, Tolstoy writes: 'A battle is won by those who are firmly resolved to win it.' We are firmly resolved to change Britain and stop Brexit. It is the only future that works. We can and must win.

What to do next

You can make a big difference.

You could start by signing up to People's Vote (www.peoples-vote.co.uk), the campaign for a people's vote on the terms of the eventual Brexit deal.
  You can also join one of the many groups battling for Britain's place in Europe.

- Best for Britain (www.bestforbritain.org) is campaigning to keep Britain in the EU, as is Britain For Europe (www.britainforeurope.org).
- Open Britain (www.open-britain.co.uk) fights against a hard and destructive Brexit.
- There is also the European Movement (www.europeanmovement.co.uk), which has been in existence for seventy years, Scientists for EU (www.scientistsforeu.uk), and Healthier IN the EU (www.healthierin.eu) for health professionals.
- Our Future, Our Choice (www.ofoc.co.uk) is a youth movement opposing Brexit. The great majority of young people do not want to leave the EU.
- Other groups provide a forum for discussion on social media, The 48%, We Are #StopBrexit, Reasons2Remain among others. There's even a group called Remainer Now for those who voted Leave but regret it. They are all on Facebook.
- If you want to get out and get active, you might join a passionate local pro-EU/anti-Brexit campaign group. Information can usually be found on Facebook. Many work tirelessly in their communities to try to persuade hearts and minds.
- SODEM (Stand of Defiance European Movement) hosts a highly visible protest outside Parliament every day that MPs are sitting: sodemaction.co.uk.
- The No10Vigil – Vigil Against Brexit (find it on Facebook) holds a protest outside Downing Street twice a week and travels to different areas at weekends.
- And if you're feeling subversive you can follow @EUFlagMafia on Twitter to see photos of EU flags hung in prominent places to demonstrate that the pro-EU voice is still alive.

  Why join any of these groups? One anti-Brexit activist said she had a love-hate relationship with Brexit. She hated it. But she loved the passion it had brought out in her and in others to fight for what she felt was the best for her country.

The truth is that no one individual can change this country's course, but together we can and we will.

Notes

Saving Britain

2 *the EU already has trade deals:* As an EU member, Britain can trade tariff-free with the twenty-seven other EU member states in the EU. The EU lists thirty-one states or territories with which it has a trade agreement, and another thirty where agreements have been provisionally applied and are being ratified by member states. In 2016, 54 per cent of British exports went to the EU and these sixty-one countries.

2 *Inward investment into the UK:* See 'Foreign Direct Investment Statistics: Data, Analysis and Forecasts', OECD.org. Inward investment fell $181 billion (£132 billion) in 2017, compared with 2016, and outward investment climbed by $120 billion (£88 billion).

1. Falling to pieces

11 *Brexit has divided the country*: Stefan Collignon, 'Brexit has the semblance of a new English Civil War', #LSEThinks blog, 9 March 2018.

12 *Of Britain's sixty-three cities*: This is the Centre for Cities definition of city.

12 *Nearly a third of Mansfield's low-skill jobs*: Centre for Cities, Cities Outlook 2018, 29 January 2018.

13 *and many more towns like them*: Boston in Lincolnshire was the town with the highest leave vote: 75.6 per cent.

14 *The richest region in Europe*: Data from Eurostat website.

14 *between 5 per cent and 30 per cent poorer*: Measured in GDP and GVA per capita.

14 *levels of interregional inequality in the UK*: McCann, *The UK*

Regional–National Economic Problem.

14 *smallest increase in the price per habitable room*: From 2004
to 2016, the house price per habitable room in London
rose from £66,717 to £132,926. By contrast, in Hartlepool
the house price per habitable room was £19,348 in 2004
and had risen by less than £500 to £19,832 in the year of
the referendum.

14 *Each person in London produces*: Andrew G. Haldane,
'Productivity Puzzles', speech at the London School of
Economics, 20 March 2017.

14 *The North-East has only a fraction*: 'North East
Independent Economic Review Report', April 2013.

15 *The euro is often criticised*: 'London and the UK: In for
a Penny, in for the Pound', Deutsche Bank Markets
Research Special Report, 27 November 2013.

15 *Though London makes up just 15 per cent*: Grace Blakeley,
'Paying for our Progress: How will the Northern Powerhouse
be Financed and Funded?', IPPR North, February 2017.

17 *'There is a fracture line running deep . . . '*: 'State of the
Nation 2017: Social Mobility in Great Britain', Social
Mobility Commission report.

18 *The now routine prescription of antidepressants*: A proportion
are literally dying from despair about their situation
and prospects – a mirror image of what is happening in
the poorest parts of the US. See Anne Case and Angus
Deaton, 'Mortality and morbidity in the 21st century',
Brookings Papers on Economic Activity Conference
Drafts, 23–24 March 2017.

18 *Deaths from liver disease alone*: 'New liver disease atlas
shows major variation across England', Public Health
England press release, 14 September 2017.

18 *half the country practically never visit the dentist*: Armstrong,
The New Poverty.

18 *There is just not the mental space*: Mullainathan and
Shafir, *Scarcity.*

18 *The life expectancy for Blackpool*: 'Life expectancy at birth and at age 65 by local areas, UK', ONS dataset, 7 December 2017.

19 *The neighbourhoods become locked into a spiral*: Glaeser and Gyourko, 'Urban Decline and Durable Housing'.

19 *'great divide'*: Goodhart, *The Road to Somewhere*.

20 *Thus football fans will be loyal*: Rod Liddle, 'Why football wants the "somewheres" to get lost', Spectator, 12 August 2017.

21 *'The nature and convertibility . . . '*: Krastev, *After Europe*.

22 *risk of top executives being viewed as 'aliens'*: Jean Eaglesham, 'CEOs risk being seen as "aliens" over pay', *Financial Times*, 30 March 2010.

23 *payment of large dividends*: See 'The collapse of Carillion', House of Commons Library research briefing, 14 March 2018.

24 *British industrialisation happened spontaneously*: Emmerich, *Britain's Cities, Britain's Future*.

25 *Lancashire industry depended heavily*: Mass and Lazonick, 'The British Cotton Industry and International Competitive Advantage'.

30 *paid less than the voluntary living wage*: Larry Elliott, 'TUC highlights UK's pay blackspots where half get less than living wage', Guardian, 1 April 2014.

30 *Half of those returning to employment*: Jacqueline O'Reilly et al., 'Brexit: understanding the socio-economic origins and consequences'.

30 *low-skilled rudimentary 'elementary' jobs*: Dorling, *Inequality and the 1%*.

30 *locked in a state of persistent poverty*: 'Persistent poverty in the UK and EU: 2015', ONS release, 27 June 2017.

31 *as estimated by the independent Office for Budget Responsibility*: Jon Riley and Robert Chote, 'Crisis and Consolidation in the Public Finances', OBR working paper 7, September 2014.

34 *immigrants from Eastern Europe*: Dustmann and Frattini, 'The Fiscal Effects of Immigration to the UK'.

34 *The Bank of England*: Stephen Nickell and Jumana Saleheen, 'The Impact of Immigration on Occupational Wages: Evidence from Britain', Bank of England working paper 574, 18 December 2015.

35 e*arn money and spend it on goods and services*: Dustmann, Frattini and Preston, 'The Effect of Immigration along the Distribution of Wages'.

35 *may have been exacerbated at the margin*: Christian Hilber, 'UK Housing and Planning Policies: the evidence from economic research', paper EA033, LSE Centre for Economic Performance 2015 Election Analyses Series.

36 *'range from somewhat negative . . . '*: Fahy et al., 'How will Brexit affect health and health services in the UK?'.

37 *by 2025 only 10 per cent of under-35s*: Adam Corlett, George Bangham and David Finch, 'The Living Standards Outlook 2018', Resolution Foundation, 22 February 2018.

38 *so the Bank of England estimates*: 'The Bank of England takes a hawkish turn', *Financial Times*, 9 February 2018.

38 *shortfall was nearer £18 billion*: Chris Giles, 'The real price of Brexit begins to emerge', *Financial Times*, 18 December 2017.

38 *set to take a disproportionate hit*: Los et al., 'The mismatch between local voting and the local economic consequences of Brexit'.

38 *EU trade arrangements cover 54 per cent*: 'Over half of UK exports were via EU trade agreements in 2016', Fullfact. org, 2 March 2018.

39 *Seventy per cent of British manufactured exports*: Peter Levell, 'Firms' supply chains form an important part of UK-EU trade: what does this mean for future trade policy?', Institute for Fiscal Studies observations, 8 January 2018.

39 *The combination of more intensive competition*: Nauro F.
    Campos, Fabrizio Coricelli and Luigi Moretti, 'Economic
    Growth and Political Integration: Estimating the Benefits
    from Membership in the European Union Using the
    Synthetic Counterfactuals Method', IZA Institute of
    Labor Economics discussion paper 8162, April 2014.

40 *The EU has been a reliable and consistent*: Tom Hunt, Scott
    Lavery, Will Vittery and Craig Berry, 'UK regions and
    European structural and investment funds', Sheffield
    Political Economy Research Institute British political
    economy brief 24, May 2016.

41 *The European Investment Bank's (EIB) lending*: 'The
    European Investment Bank in the United Kingdom: what
    we do', EIB.org.

41 *lending collapsed to £377 million*: Michael Peel, 'European
    Investment Bank lending in UK falls sharply', *Financial
    Times*, 18 January 2018.

41 *capacity to do its job is threatened*: Note that approximately
    one third of all UK nurses are due to retire in the next ten
    years. See Costa-Font, 'The National Health Service at a
    Critical Moment'.

41 *Agricultural incomes are likely to fall*: Scheherazade
    Daneshkhu, 'UK farmers risk seeing incomes halve after
    Brexit', *Financial Times*, 10 October 2017.

41 *Britain would have expected*: Authors' calculation, assuming
    EU science budget for FP 9 is €180 billion, and Britain's
    net benefit would have continued at same rate.

42 *'red tape' and ratchet up business costs*: 'The "Red Tape"
    Cost of Brexit', Oliver Wyman and Clifford Chance
    report, 2018.

43 *'This amounts to a significant . . . '*: 'UK employment rights
    and the EU: Assessment of the impact of membership of
    the European Union on employment rights in the UK',
    TUC paper.

43 *An employer planning collective redundancies*: Ibid.

44 *Recent reforms have gone some way*: Andrew Ward and Rochelle Toplensky, 'EU emissions reforms send a strong smoke signal', *Financial Times*, 9 November 2017.

44 *Similar improvements can be found*: 'Environment and climate change: review of balance of competencies', DEFRA and Department of Energy and Climate Change consultation outcome, 20 May 2013.

2. How Mr Farage became leader of the Conservative Party

47 *'We have not successfully rolled back ...'*: Margaret Thatcher, speech to the College of Europe ('The Bruges Speech'), 20 September 1988.

48 *'England in effect is insular,'*: Charles De Gaulle, veto on British membership of the EEC, 14 January 1963.

49 *It seems to me to display*: Margaret Thatcher, speech to the Conservative Group for Europe (opening Conservative referendum campaign), 16 April 1975.

50 *'single market without barriers ...'*: Margaret Thatcher, speech opening Single Market Campaign, 18 April 1988.

51 *'Cabinet now consists ...'*: Quoted in Gary Younge, 'Britain's imperial fantasies have given us Brexit', *Guardian*, 3 February 2018.

54 *'Brexit gives us a chance ...'*: Nigel Lawson, 'Brexit gives us a chance to finish the Thatcher revolution', *Financial Times*, 2 September 2016.

55 *'When I go into Downing Street ...'*: Anthony Hilton, 'Stay or go – the lack of solid facts means it's all a leap of faith', *Evening Standard*, 25 February 2016.

55 *'terrifying ... he would rampage ...'*: 'Profile: That's enough fawning on the Tories – Ed: Paul Dacre, a fresh stamp on the "Daily Mail"', *Independent*, 2 October 1992.

55 *'America taught me the power ...'*: Bill Hagerty, 'Paul Dacre: the zeal thing', *British Journalism Review*, 13:3 (2002). See also Bill Hagerty, 'Mail man', *Guardian*, 9 September 2002.

57 *In a speech drafted by Daniel Hannan*: William Hague, speech to the Conservative Spring Forum, 4 March 2001.

62 *By the time of the referendum*: See Simon Hix, Eric Kaufmann and Thomas J. Leeper, 'British voters prefer EU to non-EU migrants', #LSEThinks, 5 June 2017.

63 *'We are about to discuss ... '*: *Hansard*, vol. 759, 1241, 27 February 1968.

63 *how quickly immigration can turn toxic*: Kaufmann, 'Levels or changes?'

64 *The origins of his party*: Goodwin and Milazzo, *UKIP*.

64 *'wind-up merchant', 'bloody-minded', 'difficult'*: Farage, *The Purple Revolution*.

64 *'You've hit on the right word ... '*: 'Support for the man who will not sit', *Sunday Telegraph*, 5 June 1994.

65 *'The more I read about the history ... '*: Helen Rumbelow and Alice Miles, 'The UKIP leader, the Latvian lover and the lap dance club', *The Times*, 10 March 2007.

65 *'I was never a Tory ... '*: 'Nigel Farage: I'm the only politician keeping the flame of Thatcherism alive', *Sun*, 14 April 2013.

66 *'a parliament I want no part of ... '*: Ford and Goodwin, *Revolt on the Right*.

67 *None of this offered Farage the red meat*: Oppermann, 'The Blair Government and Europe' and Miklin, 'Beyond subsidiarity'.

67–8 *'He clearly lost the centre ground ... '*: Quoted in David Goodhart, 'Enoch Powell, the prophet of doom who clutches at us still', *Sunday Times*, 8 April 2018.

68 *'The Europhiles claim that an enlarged EU ... '*: Nigel Farage, 'Effect on UK of EU enlargement', *The Times*, 21 April 2003.

70 *Gordon Brown's disastrous encounter with Gillian Duffy*: Matthew Weaver, 'The Gordon Brown and Gillian Duffy transcript', *Guardian*, 28 April 2010.

71 *'From that day onwards ... '*: Quoted in Farrell and

Goldsmith, *How To Lose A Referendum*.

71 *'a major contributory factor...'*: '"Time for Conservative pact with Ukip", Tory campaign chief', *Evening Standard*, 26 November 2012.

72 *There was an alternative narrative*: Also see Sandbu, Europe's Orphan.

73 *'moment of near-terminal rupture'*: Sir Ivan Rogers, Hertford lecture, November 2017.

73 a *'balance of competences' review*: The review can be found at <https://www.gov.uk/guidance/review-of-the-balance-of-competences>. For commentary on the review, see Paul P. Craig, 'Brexit: A Drama in Six Acts', Oxford Legal Studies research paper 45/2016, 11 July 2016 and Emerson (ed.), *Britain's Future in Europe*.

74 *Lord Boswell put it acidly*: See 'The Review of the Balance of Competences between the UK and EU – European Union Committee', available at parliament.uk. See also Toby Helm, 'Lords accuse Tories of "burying" review that cleared EU of interference', *Guardian*, 28 March 2015.

75 *'right in principle...'*: Letwin, *Hearts and Minds*.

75 *'a tremendous victory', 'It was so obvious to me...'*: Mount, *Summer Madness*.

76 *'Mass immigration... has been all but airbrushed...'*: *Daily Mail*, 23 April 2015.

76 *'will say things that need to be said...'*: Lord Ashcroft, 'The UKIP threat is not about Europe', lordashcroftpolls.com, 18 December 2012.

78 *He even foolishly told Merkel*: Rogers, Hertford lecture.

80 *According to Survation*: Quoted in Clarke, Goodwin and Whiteley, *Brexit*.

80 *A study of 268 referendums*: Stephen Fisher and Alan Renwick, 'Do people tend to vote against change in referendums?', The Constitution Unit, UCL, 22 June 2016.

3. The lion without the roar

83 *Survey evidence finds*: James Dennison and Noah Carl, 'The ultimate causes of Brexit: history, culture, and geography', LSE Brexit blog, 18 July 2018.

84 *In polling of the wider population*: Ben Clements, Philip Lynch and Richard Whitaker, 'The low salience of European integration for British voters means that UKIP will have to expand their platform to gain more support', LSE Elections blog, 8 March 2013.

84 *It was widely held*: 'The Perils of Perception and the EU', Ipsos MORI, 9 June 2016.

85 *'What does the public see?'*: Interview, 8 December 2017.

86 *'You're not going to win here ... '*: Author interview, 2016.

87 *became the world language*: Colley, *Britons*.

87 *English history*: See Black, *Convergence or Divergence?*, Mandler, *The English National Character* and Bayly, *The Birth of the Modern World, 1780–1914*.

88 *As urban centres grew*: Findlay and O'Rourke, *Power and Plenty*.

88 *This interconnectedness has made*: Wright, *Nonzero*. See also Ghemawat, *World 3.0*.

88 *Since 1834*: 'Pooled sovereignty has advanced national goals', *Financial Times*, 12 June 2016.

92 *Adam Smith ... started writing*: Phillipson, *Adam Smith*.

92–3 *'Notwithstanding the advanced state ... '*: Hume, 'Essay VI: Of the Jealousy of Trade', *Essays*.

93 *the British proved adept at absorbing*: Mokyr, *The Enlightened Economy*. See also Zanden, *The Long Road to the Industrial Revolution*.

93 *Managing the convulsions and uncertainties*: Acemoglu and Robinson, *Economic Origins of Dictatorship and Democracy*.

93 *Beveridge, Churchill, Lloyd George*: Timmins, *The Five Giants*.

93 *'an immense historic error', 'exaggerated fears ... '*: Robert Tombs, 'The English Revolt', *New Statesman*, 24 July 2016.

95 *'Why is your chief . . . ', 'He must have repeated this . . . '*:
Winston S. Churchill, *The Second World War* (London:
Cassell & Co, 1959).

96 *For Churchill – as for Attlee*: Grob-Fitzgibbon,
Continental Drift.

96 *The first circle for us is naturally*: Winston Churchill,
Conservative mass meeting, Llandudno, 19 October
1948. See Richard Davis, 'WSC's "Three Majestic
Circles"', *Finest Hour*, 160 (autumn 2013).

97 *'We are prepared to consider . . . '*: *Hansard*, vol. 476, 2043,
26 June 1950.

97 *'There are disadvantages . . . '*: Winston S. Churchill,
Stemming the Tide (London: Cassell, 1953).

99 *Britain built its overseas possessions*: Simms,
Britain's Europe.

99 *Citizens – and ominously younger voters*: Foa and Mounk,
'The Democratic Disconnect'.

99 *Not intelligence collection, but subversion*: Quoted in
Shekhovtsov, *Russia and the Western Far Right*.

4. Get real

103 *No country in today's world*: Rodrik, *The
Globalization Paradox*.

106 *The opinion-poll evidence*: Marley Morris, 'Leaving
the EU, Not the European Model? New Findings on
Public Attitudes to Brexit (Part One)', IPPR briefing,
February 2018.

106 *financial services and the City of London*: Armour, 'Brexit
and Financial Services'.

107 *Such is the volume of lorries*: James Blitz, 'Why Dover is
braced for customs gridlock after Brexit', *Financial Times*,
18 October 2017. On the viability of technology-based
solutions, see Joe Owen, Marcus Shepheard and Alex
Stojanovic, 'Implementing Brexit: Customs', Institute for
Government analysis, September 2017.

107   *Britain's imports of fresh food*: Ben Chapman, 'Brexit
      Britain at risk from food shortages, rising prices and
      lower animal welfare standards, hears Lords committee',
      Independent, 7 February 2018.

109   *Moreover, the UK has rarely been outvoted*: Simon Hix and
      Sara Hagemann, 'Does the UK win or lose in the Council
      of Ministers?', LSE Brexit blog, 2 November 2015.

110   *Few Americans are aware*: Bradford, 'The Brussels Effect'.

112   *a mere 2.8 per cent*: The equivalent rate for the US is 2.7
      per cent. Needless to say, the EU has preferential trade
      arrangements with other countries granting duty-free and
      quota-free access to the EU. This includes many raw and
      processed goods from the developing world under the
      Everything but Arms agreements.

113–14 *Britain should pivot*: On the perils of extrapolating
      past growth rates, see Lant Pritchett and Lawrence H.
      Summers, 'Asiaphoria Meets Regression to the Mean',
      NBER working paper 20573, October 2014.

114   *Of 101 middle-income economies*: Agénor, Canuto and
      Jelenic, 'Avoiding Middle-Income Growth Traps'.

114   *Over the last decade*: Cristina Constantinescu, Aaditya
      Mattoo and Michele Ruta, 'The Global Trade Slowdown:
      Cyclical or Structural?', IMF working paper WP/15/6.

114   *so the IMF calculates*: 'Europe: Engine for Global Trade,
      but Should Prepare for Rainy Day', IMF country focus, 13
      November 2017.

114   *The UK share of EU exports to India*: Maria Demertzis and
      Alexander Roth, 'India's trade ties with the UK and EU',
      Bruegel.org blog, 6 October 2017.

115   *Brexit economist Patrick Minford*: See Thomas Sampson,
      Swati Dhingra, Gianmarco Ottaviano and John Van
      Reenen, 'Economists for Brexit: A Critique', LSE Centre
      for Economic Performance Brexit analysis 6, 21 August
      2017, and L. Alan Winters, 'Will eliminating UK tariffs
      boost UK GDP by 4 percent? Even "Economists for Free

Trade" don't believe it!', UK Trade Policy Observatory blog, 19 April 2017.

115 *Every study on trade*: Keith Head and Thierry Mayer, 'Gravity Equations: Workhorse, Toolkit, and Cookbook', Centre d'Études Prospectives et d'Informations Internationales working paper 2013.

115 *global supply chain that dictates*: James E. Anderson and Eric van Wincoop, 'Trade Costs', NBER working paper 10480, May 2004; Johnson and Noguera, 'Accounting for intermediates'; and 'World Investment Report 2013: Global Value Chains: Investment and Trade for Development', UNCTAD.

115 *you cannot abolish distance*: McCallum, 'National Borders Matter', and James E. Anderson and Eric van Wincoop, 'Gravity with Gravitas: A Solution to the Border Puzzle', NBER working paper 8079, January 2001.

115 *The single market has created*: 'Review of the Balance of Competences between the United Kingdom and the European Union: The Single Market', HM Government report, July 2013.

116 *'Today it is "European" ... '*: Initial Vodafone comments on FCO Balance of Competences Review, 'Submissions to the Call for Evidence – HMG Review of the Balance of Competencies between the UK and EU Internal Market: Synoptic Review'.

116 *Theresa May recognised as much*: See Tom Peck, 'Sketch: Theresa May gives a speech she hopes you will have already forgotten', *Independent*, 25 April 2016.

117 *Concluding FTAs*: Ebell, 'Assessing the Impact of Trade Agreements on Trade'.

117 If Britain secures a preferential: Alen Mulabdic, Alberto Osnago and Michele Ruta, 'Deep Integration and UK–EU Trade Relations', World Bank policy research working paper 7947, January 2017.

118 *'It is rejecting a three-course meal ... '*: Comments on BBC

Radio 4 Today programme, 27 February 2018.

118 *usually imposed by strong powers*: Palem, *The 'Conspiracy' of Free Trade* and Chang, *Kicking Away the Ladder*.

119 *One estimate suggests*: Peter Levell, 'The Customs Union, tariff reductions and consumer prices', Institute for Fiscal Studies briefing note BN225, 20 March 2018. The estimate is optimistic because it assumes perfect competition in product markets and perfect substitutability between imported and domestic goods, meaning that UK firms and foreign exporters have no scope to raise prices. It also assumes that wholesalers pass on the entirety of the reduced costs to consumers.

120 *costs of up to £27 billion*: 'The "Red Tape" Cost of Brexit', Oliver Wyman and Clifford Chance report, 2018.

120 *Both the US and China*: Pankaj Mishra, 'The Rise of China and the Fall of the "Free Trade" Myth', *New York Times Magazine*, 7 February 2018, and Robert W. Merry, 'America's History of Protectionism', *The National Interest*, 18 October 2016.

122 *While Switzerland had to open its markets*: Swati Dhingra and Nikhil Datta, 'How Not to Do Trade Deals', *London Review of Books*, 39:18 (21 September 2017)

124 *People employed in public-sector jobs*: Sadiq Khan, 'London Mayor Sadiq Khan: Time to let go of segregation – globally', *Chicago Tribune*, 14 September 2016.

125 *Survey evidence shows*: Eric Kaufmann, 'Assimilation and the immigration debate: shifting people's attitudes', LSE Economy & Society blog, 1 October 2016.

127 *£140 million over the four years*: Melanie Gower, 'The new Controlling Migration Fund for England', House of Commons briefing paper 7673, 7 December 2017.

5. Stakeholder capitalism and the new social contract

132   *lack of public institutions to support growth*: Letter from
      John Cridland, Director-General of the CBI, to George
      Osborne, Chancellor of the Exchequer, 25 February 2015.

133   *They paid £83 billion of taxes*: '2017 Total Tax Contribution
      survey for the 100 Group: A sustained contribution in
      uncertain times', PwC report, December 2017.

134   *Alarmism that digitalisation*: Bakhshi, Downing, Osborne
      and Schneider, *The Future of Skills*.

136   *Dresden's Max Planck Institute*: van Agtmael and Bakker,
      The Smartest Places on Earth.

136   *'the entrepreneurial state'*: Mazzucato, *The
      Entrepreneurial State*.

138   *So high is the number of low-performing firms*: OECD, *The
      Future of Productivity* (2015).

138   *There is also scope for radial gains*: Justin Bentham et al.,
      'Manifesto for the Foundational Economy', Centre for
      Research on Socio-Cultural Change working paper 131,
      November 2013.

138   *Retail and hospitality alone*: Daniel Wright and Rachel
      Case, 'Industrial Strategy must improve prospects of
      poorest places post Brexit', Joseph Rowntree Foundation,
      17 April 2017.

139   *Evidence assembled by the Big Innovation Centre*: 'The
      Purposeful Company: Interim Report', May 2016.

142   *Companies need 'anchored' shareholders*: Alex Edmans
      and Clifford G. Holderness, 'Blockholders: A Survey of
      Theory and Evidence', European Corporate Governance
      Institute finance working paper 475/2016, 13 August 2016.

144   *Mutually owned Employee Ownership Trusts*: Mathew
      Lawrence and Nigel Mason, 'Capital Gains: Broadening
      company ownership in the UK economy', IPPR
      Commission on Economic Justice policy paper,
      December 2017.

145   *Long-term stewardship of companies*: Gavin Jackson,

'Who owns Britain's companies?', *Financial Times*, 27 January 2016.

145 *In any case, many of the forty thousand pension funds*: Contrast the situation with the US: Webber, *The Rise of the Working-Class Shareholder*.

145 *A Citizens' Wealth Fund should be created*: Carys Roberts and Mathew Lawrence, 'Our Common Wealth: A Citizens' Wealth Fund for the UK', IPPR Commission on Economic Justice policy paper, April 2018.

146 *Analogue capitalism is also consolidating*: David Autor, David Dorn, Lawrence F. Katz, Christina Patterson and John Van Reenen, ''The Fall of the Labor Share and the Rise of Superstar Firms', LSE Centre for Economic Performance discussion paper 1482, May 2017; and Scott Corfe and Nicole Gicheva, 'Concentration not competition: the state of UK consumer markets', Social Market Foundation, October 2017.

147 *Amazon secures extortionate discounts*: Lina M. Khan, 'Amazon's Antitrust Paradox', *Yale Law Journal*, 126:3 (January 2017).

147 *Uber is burning through investors' cash*: Michael Haupt, 'Can Uber Ever Deliver? An analysis of Uber's staggering unprofitability', Medium.com, 25 February 2017; and Murray Goulden, 'Uber can't be ethical – its business model won't allow it', TheConversation.com, 4 October 2017.

147 *Facebook is siphoning advertising*: Foer, *World Without Mind*.

147 *Facebook has bought WhasApp, Microsoft owns LinkedIn*: Tim Cowen and Phillip Blond, 'Markets and the New Monopolies', Big Innovation Centre and ResPublica, May 2018.

148 *Yet without the challenge of new entrants*: Germán Gutiérrez and Thomas Philipon, 'Investmentless Growth: An Empirical Investigation', Brookings Papers on Economic Activity Conference Drafts, 7–8 September 2017.

148 *'The company made the decision ... '*: Evelyn M. Rusli, 'Google's Deal-Making Math', *New York Times*, 8 July 2011.

150 *Less than 15 per cent*: 'Trade Union Membership 2016', Department for Business, Energy and Industrial Strategy statistical bulletin, May 2017.

150 *Because there are few strong private-sector unions*: Weil, *The Fissured Workplace* and Fichtenbaum, 'Do Unions Affect Labor's Share of Income'.

150 *Unions need reinventing*: The proposals draw on work by the Fabian Society: Cameron Tait, 'Future Unions: Towards a membership renaissance in the private sector', November 2017.

154 *The NHS budget*: Martin Wolf, 'The expensive truth about high-quality healthcare', *Financial Times*, 22 February 2018.

155 *The National Infrastructure Commission has identified*: 'Adonis and business leaders urge Government to press ahead rapidly with key infrastructure plans', National Infrastructure Commission, 20 June 2017.

157 *The IMF finds no evidence*: 'IMF Fiscal Monitor: Tackling Inequality, October 2017'.

157 *Nor is there evidence that lowering already-low corporation tax*: Nir Jaimovich and Sergio Rebelo, 'Non-linear Effects of Taxation on Growth', NBER working paper 18473, October 2012.

157 *fair taxation of property*: Collins, Lloyd and Macfarlane, *Rethinking the Economics of Land and Housing*.

159 *Inheritance tax has become a voluntary tax*: 'The Role and Design of Net Wealth Taxes in the OECD', OECD tax policy studies, 12 April 2018.

161 *disproportionate number of whom are educated privately*: 'Elitist Britain?', Social Mobility and Child Poverty Commission report.

162 *decent apprenticeships for less than half*: Brinkley and Crowley, 'From "inadequate" to "outstanding"'.

164 *The one unambiguously successful initiative*: Professor Alison
     Wolf with Gerard Domínguez-Reig and Peter Sellen,
     'Remaking Tertiary Education: can we create a system
     that is fair and fit for purpose?', Education Policy Institute
     report, November 2016.
164 *In 2016, a third of five-year-olds*: 'Bold beginnings:
     'The Reception curriculum in a sample of good and
     outstanding primary schools', Ofsted report 170045,
     November 2017.

6. Taking back real control

169 *'a failure of citizenship'*: Remarks to author. See also Ben
     Okri, 'How to combat the populism that gave us Brexit?
     Active citizenship', *Guardian*, 30 January 2018.
172–3 *Magna Carta is one of a European family*: Jeremy Catto,
     'Magna Carta and the Origins of Freedom and Democracy',
     The Foundation of Liberty: Magna Carta after 800 Years,
     Hoover Institution conference, 25 June 2015.
174 *The new reality is extreme partisan polarisation*: Levitsky
     and Ziblatt, *How Democracies Die*.
176–7 *The growth of the state*: Tombs, *The English and their History*.
185 *Apart from London and perhaps Birmingham and
     Manchester/Salford*: McCann, The UK Regional–National
     Economic Problem and Henry Overman, 'The UK's
     Regional Divide: Can Policy Make a Difference?', LSE
     Centre for Economic Performance 2015 Election Analyses
     Series paper EA042.
186 *International evidence is that*: Chetty, Hendren, Kline and
     Saez, 'Where is the Land of Opportunity'.
187 *Worst-placed are the isolated small cities*: This builds on the
     typology developed by the Joseph Rowntree Foundation:
     Andy Pike et al., 'Uneven growth: tackling city decline',
     March 2016.
194 *Research has found that fake news*: Lazer et al., 'The science
     of fake news'.

7. Statues of liberty

196 *Echoes of the years before 1914*: Clark, *The Sleepwalkers*.

196 *There is a clear fault line*: Ivor Roberts, 'The west must not just abandon the Balkans to Russia's embrace', *Guardian*, 5 April 2018.

196 *His twenty-year reign*: Snyder, *The Road to Unfreedom*.

197 *'We are in a new era ...'*: Madeleine Albright, 'Will We Stop Trump Before It's Too Late?', *New York Times*, 6 April 2018.

197 *'Russia makes little secret ...'*: Roberts, 'The west must not just abandon the Balkans to Russia's embrace'.

198 *Had I been cryogenically frozen*: Timothy Garton Ash, 'Is Europe Disintegrating?', *New York Review of Books*, 19 January 2017.

199 *when Nigel Farage welcomed*: Ibid.

203 *General Petr Pavel*: Paul McLeary, 'Top NATO General (A Czech) To Europe: "Grow Up"', breakingdefense.com, 7 March 2018.

204 *has no time for 'EUroids'*: Bolton, *Surrender Is Not an Option*.

204 *Countries that engage in trade wars*: Marc-William Palen, 'Protectionism 100 years ago helped ignite a world war. Could it happen again?', *Washington Post*, 30 June 2017.

206 *China's President Xi represents a threat*: Allison, *Destined for War*.

207 *'We can't pretend ...'*: Simon Heffer, 'We can't pretend it didn't happen', *Daily Telegraph*, 24 March 2018.

208 *'the Anglo-Irish story ...'*: Ibid.

211 *'We have many theories ...'*: Zielonka, *Is the EU Doomed?*

214 *The UK controls more than 98 per cent*: Albright, 'Will We Stop Trump Before It's Too Late?'

Bibliography

Acemoglu, Daron and James A. Robinson, *Economic Origins of Dictatorship and Democracy: Economic and Political Origins* (Cambridge: Cambridge University Press, 2005)

Agénor, Pierre-Richard, Otaviano Canuto and Michael Jelenic, 'Avoiding Middle-Income Growth Traps', *Economic Premise*, 98 (2012)

Agtmael, Antoine van and Fred Bakker, *The Smartest Places on Earth: Why Rustbelts Are the Emerging Hotspots of Global Innovation* (New York: Public Affairs, 2016)

Allison, Graham, *Destined for War: Can America and China Escape Thucydides' Trap?* (London: Scribe, 2017)

Armour, John, 'Brexit and Financial Services', *Oxford Review of Economic Policy*, Brexit Special Issue (forthcoming)

Armstrong, Stephen, *The New Poverty* (London: Verso, 2017)

Aussilloux, Vincent, Agnès Bénassy-Quéré, Clemens Fuest and Guntram Wolff, 'Making the best of the European single market', *Policy Contribution*, 3 (2017)

Autor, David, David Dorn, Gordon Hanson and Kaveh Majlesi, 'Importing Political Polarization? The Electoral Consequences of Rising Trade Exposure', NBER working paper 22637 (2017)

Bakhshi, Hasan, Jonathan M. Downing, Michael A. Osborne and Philippe Schneider, *The Future of Skills: Employment in 2030* (London: Pearson and Nesta, 2017)

Baldwin, Richard, *The Great Convergence: Information Technology*

and the New Globalization (Cambridge, MA: Harvard
University Press, 2016)

Bayly, C. A., *The Birth of the Modern World, 1780–1914: Global
Connections and Comparisons* (Oxford: Blackwell, 2004)

Becker, Sascha O., Erik Hornung and Ludger Woessmann,
'Education and Catch-Up in the Industrial Revolution',
American Economic Journal: Macroeconomics, 3:3 (2011)

Birkinshaw, Patrick J. and Andrea Biondi (eds), *Britain Alone! The
Implications and Consequences of United Kingdom Exit from the
EU* (Alphen aan den Rijn: Kluwer Law International, 2016)

Black, Jeremy, *Convergence or Divergence?: Britain and the
Continent* (Basingstoke: Palgrave, 1994)

Bolton, John, *Surrender Is Not an Option: Defending America at the
United Nations and Abroad* (New York: Threshold Editions, 2008)

Bradford, Anu, 'The Brussels Effect', *Northwestern Law Review*,
107:1 (2012)

Brinkley, Ian Elizabeth Crowley, 'From "inadequate" to
"outstanding": making the UK's skills system world class',
CIPD (2017)

Brunnermeier, Markus K., Harold James and Jean-Pierre
Landau, *The Euro and the Battle of Ideas* (Princeton: Princeton
University Press, 2016)

Chang, Ha-Joon, *Kicking Away the Ladder: Development Strategy in
Historical Perspective* (London: Anthem, 2003)

Chetty, Raj, Nathaniel Hendren, Patrick Kline and Emmanuel
Saez, 'Where is the Land of Opportunity: The Geography
of Intergenerational Mobility in the United States', *Quarterly
Journal of Economics*, 129:4 (2014)

Clark, Christopher, *The Sleepwalkers: How Europe Went to War in
1914* (London: Allen Lane, 2012)

Clark, Greg, *The Making of a World City: London 1991 to 2021*
     (Chichester: Wiley-Blackwell, 2015)

Clarke, Harold D., Matthew Goodwin and Paul Whiteley, *Brexit:
     Why Britain Voted to Leave the European Union* (Cambridge:
     Cambridge University Press, 2017)

Colantone, Italo and Piero Stanig, 'Global Competition and
     Brexit', BAFFI CAREFIN research paper 2016-44 (2016)

Colley, Linda, *Britons: Forging the Nation 1707–1837* (New Haven:
     Yale University Press, 2009)

Collins, Josh Ryan, Toby Lloyd and Laurie Macfarlane,
     Rethinking the Economics of Land and Housing (London: Zed
     Books, 2017)

Costa-Font, Joan, 'The National Health Service at a Critical
     Moment: when Brexit means Hectic', *Journal of Social Policy*,
     46:4 (2017)

Dewey, John (ed. Melvin L. Rogers), *The Public and Its Problems: An
     Essay in Political Inquiry* (Athens: Ohio University Press, 2016)

Dorling, Danny, *Inequality and the 1%* (London: Verso, 2015)

Dustmann, Christian and Tommaso Frattini, 'The Fiscal Effects
     of Immigration to the UK', *The Economic Journal*, 124:580
     (November 2014)

————, Tommaso Frattini and Ian P. Preston, 'The Effect
     of Immigration along the Distribution of Wages', *Review of
     Economic Studies*, 80:1 (2013)

Ebell, Monique, 'Assessing the Impact of Trade Agreements on
     Trade', *National Institute Economic Review*, 238:1 (2016)

Emerson, Michael (ed.), *Britain's Future in Europe: Reform,
     renegotiation, repatriation or secession?* (London: Rowman &
     Littlefield International, 2015)

Emmerich, Mike, *Britain's Cities, Britain's Future* (London:

London Publishing Partnership, 2017)

Farage, Nigel, *The Purple Revolution: The Year That Changed Everything* (London: Biteback, 2015)

Farrell, Jason and Paul Goldsmith, *How To Lose A Referendum: The Definitive Story of Why the UK Voted for Brexit* (London: Biteback, 2017)

Fichtenbaum, Rudy Fichtenbaum, 'Do Unions Affect Labor's Share of Income: Evidence Using Panel Data', *American Journal of Economics and Sociology*, 7:3 (2011)

Findlay, Ronald and Kevin H. O'Rourke, *Power and Plenty: Trade, War, and the World Economy in the Second Millennium* (Princeton: Princeton University Press, 2007)

Foa, Roberto Stefan and Yascha Mounk, 'The Democratic Disconnect', *Journal of Democracy*, 27:3 (2016)

Foer, Franklin, *World Without Mind: The Existential Threat of Big Tech* (London: Penguin, 2017)

Ford, Robert and Matthew J. Goodwin, *Revolt on the Right: Explaining Support for the Radical Right in Britain* (Abingdon: Routledge, 2014)

Ghemawat, Pankaj, *World 3.0: Global Prosperity and How to Achieve It* (Boston: Harvard Business School Press, 2011)

Glaeser, Edward L. and Joseph Gyourko, 'Urban Decline and Durable Housing', *Journal of Political Economy*, 112:2 (2005)

Goldstein, Amy, *Janesville: An American Story* (New York: Simon & Schuster, 2017)

Goodhart, David, *The Road to Somewhere: The Populist Revolt and the Future of Politics* (London: C. Hurst & Co, 2017)

Goodwin, Matthew and Caitlin Milazzo, *UKIP: Inside the Campaign to Redraw the Map of British Politics* (Oxford: Oxford University Press, 2015)

Grob-Fitzgibbon, Benjamin, *Continental Drift: Britain and Europe from the End of Empire to the Rise of Euroscepticism* (Cambridge: Cambridge University Press, 2016)

Halligan, Liam and Gerard Lyons, *Clean Brexit: Why Leaving the EU Still Makes Sense* (London: Biteback, 2017)

Hastings, Adrian, *The Construction of Nationhood: Ethnicity, Religion and Nationalism* (Cambridge: Cambridge University Press, 1997)

Hume, David, *Essays, Moral, Political, and Literary* (1742)

Johnson, Robert C. and Guillermo Noguera, 'Accounting for intermediates: Production sharing and trade in value added', *Journal of International Economics*, 86:2 (M2012)

Judt, Tony, *Postwar: A History of Europe Since 1945* (London: Heinemann, 2005)

Kaufmann, Eric, 'Levels or changes? Ethnic context, immigration and the UK Independence party vote', *Electoral Studies*, 48 (2017)

Kenny, Michael, *The Politics of English Nationhood* (Oxford: Oxford University Press, 2014)

Khan, Lina M., 'Amazon's Antitrust Paradox', *Yale Law Journal*, 126:3 (January 2017)

Krastev, Ivan, *Democracy Disrupted: The Politics of Global Protest* (Philadelphia: University of Pennsylvania Press, 2014)
————, *After Europe* (Philadelphia: University of Pennsylvania Press, 2017)

Lazer, David M. J. et al., 'The science of fake news', *Science*, 359:6380 (2018)

Letwin, Oliver Letwin, *Hearts and Minds: The Battle for the Conservative Party from Thatcher to the present* (London: Biteback, 2017)

Levitsky, Steven and Daniel Ziblatt, *How Democracies Die: What History Reveals About Our Future* (London: Penguin, 2018)

Los, Bart, Philip McCann, John Springfield and Mark Thissen, 'The mismatch between local voting and the local economic consequences of Brexit', *Regional Studies*, 51:5 (2017)

Mandler, Peter, *The English National Character: The History of an Idea from Edmund Burke to Tony Blair* (New Haven: Yale University Press, 2006)

Mass, William and William Lazonick, 'The British Cotton Industry and International Competitive Advantage: The State of the Debates', *Business History*, 32:4 (1990)

Mazzucato, Mariana, *The Entrepreneurial State: Debunking Public vs. Private Sector Myths* (London: Anthem, 2013)

——————, *The Value of Everything: Making and Taking in the Global Economy* (London: Allen Lane, 2018)

McCallum, John, 'National Borders Matter: Canada–US Regional Trade Patterns', *American Economic Review*, 85:3 (1995)

McCann, Philip, *The UK Regional–National Economic Problem: Geography, globalisation and governance (Regions and Cities)* (Abingdon: Routledge, 2016)

Miklin, Eric, 'Beyond subsidiarity: the indirect effect of the Early Warning System on national parliamentary scrutiny in European Union affairs', *Journal of European Public Policy*, 24:3 (2017)

Mokyr, Joel, *The Enlightened Economy: Britain and the Industrial Revolution 1700–1850* (New Haven: Yale University Press, 2009)

Moore, Charles, *Margaret Thatcher: The Authorized Biography, Volume One: Not For Turning* (London: Allen Lane, 2013)

——————, *Margaret Thatcher: The Authorized Biography, Volume Two: Everything She Wants* (London: Allen Lane, 2015)

Mount, Harry, *Summer Madness: How Brexit Split the Tories, Destroyed Labour and Divided the Country* (London: Biteback, 2017)

Mullainathan, Sendhil and Eldar Shafir, *Scarcity: Why Having Too Little Means So Much* (London: Penguin, 2013)

Murphy, Philip, *The Empire's New Clothes: The Myth of the Commonwealth* (London: Hurst, 2018)

Nick Fahy et al., 'How will Brexit affect health and health services in the UK? Evaluating three possible scenarios', *Lancet*, 390:10107 (2017)

O'Reilly, Jacqueline et al., 'Brexit: understanding the socio-economic origins and consequences', *Socio-Economic Review*, 14:4 (2016)

Oppermann, Kai, 'The Blair Government and Europe: The Policy of Containing the Salience of European Integration', *British Politics*, 3:2 (2008)

Overy, Richard, *Why The Allies Won* (London: Pimlico, 1995)

Palem, Marc-William, *The 'Conspiracy' of Free Trade: The Anglo-American Struggle over Empire and Economic Globalisation, 1846–1896* (Cambridge: Cambridge University Press, 2016)

Pettis, Michael, *The Great Rebalancing: Trade, Conflict, and the Perilous Road Ahead for the World Economy* (Princeton: Princeton University Press, 2013)

Phillipson, Nicholas, *Adam Smith: An Enlightened Life* (London: Allen Lane, 2010)

Piketty, Thomas (trans. Arthur Goldhammer), *Capital in the Twenty-First Century* (Cambridge, MA: The Belknap Press of Harvard University, 2014)

Rodrik, Dani, *The Globalization Paradox* (Oxford: Oxford University Press, 2002)

——————, 'Premature Deindustrialization', NBER working paper 20935 (2015)

Sandbu, Martin, *Europe's Orphan: The Future of the Euro and the Politics of Debt* (Princeton: Princeton University Press, 2015)

Scales, Len and Oliver Zimmer (eds), *Power and the Nation in European History* (Cambridge: Cambridge University Press, 2005)

Scheidel, Walter, *The Great Leveler: Violence and the History of Inequality from the Stone Age to the Twenty-First Century* (Princeton: Princeton University Press, 2017)

Shekhovtsov, Anton, *Russia and the Western Far Right: Tango Noir* (Abingdon: Routledge, 2017)

Shipman, Tim, *All Out War: The Full Story of How Brexit Sank Britain's Political Class* (London: William Collins, 2016)

——————, *Fall Out: A Year of Political Mayhem* (London: William Collins, 2017)

Simms, Brendan, *Britain's Europe: A Thousand Years of Conflict and Cooperation* (London: Penguin, 2016)

Snyder, Timothy, *The Road to Unfreedom: Russia, Europe, America* (London: Bodley Head, 2018)

Thatcher, Margaret, *Statecraft: Strategies for a Changing World* (London: HarperCollins, 2011)

Timmins, Nicholas, *The Five Giants: A Biography of the Welfare State* (1995; London: HarperCollins, 2001)

Tombs, Robert, *The English and their History* (London: Allen Lane, 2014)

Webber, David, *The Rise of the Working-Class Shareholder: Labor's Best Weapon* (Cambridge, MA: Harvard University Press, 2018)

Weil, David Weil, *The Fissured Workplace: Why Work Became So Bad for So Many and What Can Be Done to Improve It* (Cambridge, MA: Harvard University Press, 2017)

Wilkinson, Richard and Kate Pickett, *The Spirit Level: Why Equality is Better for Everyone* (London: Penguin, 2010)

Williams, Joan C., *White Working Class: Overcoming Class Cluelessness in America* (Boston: Harvard Business Review Press, 2017)

Wright, Robert, *Nonzero: History, Evolution & Human Cooperation* (London: Little, Brown, 2000)

Zanden, Jan Luiten van, *The Long Road to the Industrial Revolution: The European Economy in Global Perspective* (Leiden: Brill, 2009)

Zielonka, Jan, *Counter-Revolution: Liberal Europe in Retreat* (Oxford: Oxford University Press, 2018)

Zielonka, Jan, *Is the EU Doomed?* (Cambridge: Polity, 2014)